BTEC Level 2 Technical Certificate

Business Administration

Learner Handbook

Bethan Bithell
Vaughan Downes
Kath Greyner
Elaine Jackson

Published by Pearson Education Limited, 80 Strand, London, WC2R 0RL.

www.pearsonschoolsandfecolleges.co.uk

Copies of official specifications for all Pearson qualifications may be found on the website: qualifications.pearson.com

Text © Pearson Education Ltd 2017
Edited by Cambridge Publishing Management Ltd
Typeset by Phoenix Photosetting, Chatham, Kent, UK
Original illustrations © Pearson Education Ltd 2017
Illustrated by Phoenix Photosetting, Chatham, Kent, UK *and* Tech-Set Ltd
Cover photo/illustration © Rawpixel.com / Shutterstock.com

The rights of Bethan Bithell, Vaughan Downes, Kath Greyner and Elaine Jackson to be identified as authors of this work have been asserted by them in accordance with the Copyright, Designs and Patents Act 1988.

First published 2017

19 18
10 9 8 7 6 5 4

British Library Cataloguing in Publication Data
A catalogue record for this book is available from the British Library

ISBN 978 1 292 19769 2

Copyright notice
All rights reserved. No part of this publication may be reproduced in any form or by any means (including photocopying or storing it in any medium by electronic means and whether or not transiently or incidentally to some other use of this publication) without the written permission of the copyright owner, except in accordance with the provisions of the Copyright, Designs and Patents Act 1988 or under the terms of a licence issued by the Copyright Licensing Agency, Barnards Inn, 86 Fetter Lane, London EC4A 1EN (www.cla.co.uk). Applications for the copyright owner's written permission should be addressed to the publisher.

Printed in the UK by CPI

Acknowledgements

The authors and publisher would like to thank the following individuals and organisations for permission to reproduce photographs:

(Key: b-bottom; c-centre; l-left; r-right; t-top)

123RF.com: 90, 97, 106, 114t, 114b, 141tc, nexusplexus 79, petro 159, rawpixel 59, stockbroker 77; **Alamy Stock Photo:** Andreas Berheide 74, BSIP SA 11, Nick David 16, Hero Images Inc. 115, Jon Parker Lee 69tl, charoen pattarapitak 69tr, PhotoAlto 52, Rawpixel 150, Lynne Sutherland 14, SFL Travel 34; **Fotolia.com:** aleutie 155, chrisdorney 66, Elnur 69bl, julief514 10, Natis 141bc, Balint Radu 140, rilueda 138, Stokkete 75, Studio M 69br; **Getty Images:** Sydney Roberts 2; **Pearson Education Ltd:** Coleman Yuen. Pearson Education Asia Ltd 12, David Sanderson 71, Studio 8 54; **Plain English Campaign:** 22; **Shutterstock.com:** 76219 88, Sylvie Bouchard 9, Corepics VOF 23, Ditty_about_summer 93, EDHAR 152, Kekyalyaynen 5, Kzenon 31, Monkey Business Images 25, 82, Monkey Business Images 25, 82, Dmitry Naumov 165, Tyler Olson 62, Marko Poplasen 141b, Pressmaster 104, 110r, 128, Pressmaster 104, 110r, 128, Rawpixel.com 120, roilir 108, Scanrail1 95, Alex Staroseltsev. 141t, Mila Supinskaya Glashchenko 110l, Icons vector 107, Winui 131

Cover image: *Front:* **Shutterstock.com:** Rawpixel.com

Websites
Pearson Education Limited is not responsible for the content of any external internet sites. It is essential for tutors to preview each website before using it in class so as to ensure that the URL is still accurate, relevant and appropriate. We suggest that tutors bookmark useful websites and consider enabling students to access them through the school/college intranet.

Notes from the publisher
1.
In order to ensure that this resource offers high-quality support for the associated Pearson qualification, it has been through a review process by the awarding body. This process confirms that this resource fully covers the teaching and learning content of the specification or part of a specification at which it is aimed. It also confirms that it demonstrates an appropriate balance between the development of subject skills, knowledge and understanding, in addition to preparation for assessment.

Endorsement does not cover any guidance on assessment activities or processes (e.g. practice questions or advice on how to answer assessment questions), included in the resource nor does it prescribe any particular approach to the teaching or delivery of a related course.

While the publishers have made every attempt to ensure that advice on the qualification and its assessment is accurate, the official specification and associated assessment guidance materials are the only authoritative source of information and should always be referred to for definitive guidance.

Pearson examiners have not contributed to any sections in this resource relevant to examination papers for which they have responsibility.

Examiners will not use endorsed resources as a source of material for any assessment set by Pearson.

Endorsement of a resource does not mean that the resource is required to achieve this Pearson qualification, nor does it mean that it is the only suitable material available to support the qualification, and any resource lists produced by the awarding body shall include this and other appropriate resources.

2.
Pearson has robust editorial processes, including answer and fact checks, to ensure the accuracy of the content in this publication, and every effort is made to ensure this publication is free of errors. We are, however, only human, and occasionally errors do occur. Pearson is not liable for any misunderstandings that arise as a result of errors in this publication, but it is our priority to ensure that the content is accurate. If you spot an error, please do contact us at resourcescorrections@pearson.com so we can make sure it is corrected.

Contents

How to use this book		iv
1 Understanding Administrative Services	Vaughan Downes	**2**
Answers		51
2 Providing Administrative Services	Bethan Bithell	**52**
3 Using Business Technology to Process and Communicate Information	Elaine Jackson	**88**
4 Planning, Organising and Supporting Business Events	Kath Greyner	**128**
Glossary		175
Index		178

How to use this book

This handbook is designed to support you in developing the skills and knowledge to succeed in your BTEC Level 2 Technical course. It will help you to feel confident in taking the next step and be ready for your dream job.

The skills you will develop during the course include practical skills that you'll need in your chosen occupation, as well as a range of 'transferable' skills and behaviours that will be useful for your own personal development, whatever you do in life.

Your learning can be seen as a journey which moves through four phases.

Phase 1	Phase 2	Phase 3	Phase 4
You are introduced to a topic or concept; you start to develop an awareness of what learning and skills are required.	You explore the topic or concept through different methods (e.g. watching or listening to a tutor or a professional at work, research, questioning, analysis, critical evaluation) and form your own understanding.	You apply your knowledge and skills to a practical task designed to demonstrate your understanding and skills.	You reflect on your learning, evaluate your efforts, identify gaps in your knowledge and look for ways to improve.

During each phase, you will use different learning strategies. As you go through your course, these strategies will combine to help you secure the essential knowledge and skills.

This handbook has been written using similar learning principles, strategies and tools. It has been designed to support your learning journey, to give you control over your own learning and to equip you with the knowledge, understanding and tools to be successful in your future career or studies.

Getting to know the features

In this handbook you'll find lots of different features. They are there to help you learn about the topics in your course in different ways and to help you monitor and check your progress. Together these features help you:

- build your knowledge and technical skills
- understand how to succeed in your assessment
- link your learning to the workplace.

In addition, each individual feature has a specific purpose, designed to support important learning strategies. For example, some features will:

- get you to question assumptions around what you are learning
- make you think beyond what you are reading about
- help you make connections across your learning and across units
- draw comparisons between the theory you are learning about and realistic workplace environments
- help you develop some of the important skills you will need for the workplace, including planning and completing tasks, working with others, effective communication, adaptability and problem solving.

Features to build your knowledge and technical skills

Key terms

Terms highlighted like this are '**KEY TERMS**'. It is important that you know what they mean because they relate directly to your chosen subject. The first time they appear in the book they will be explained. If you see a highlighted key term again after that and can't quite remember its definition, look in the Glossary towards the end of the book – they are all listed there! Note that these key terms are used and explained in the context of your specialist subject or the topic in which they appear, and are not necessarily the same definitions you would find in a dictionary.

Practise

These work-related tasks or activities will allow you to practise some of the technical or professional skills relating to the main content covered in each unit.

> **Practise**
>
> Produce an A4 poster to display in your workplace that outlines good time management tips.

Skills and knowledge check

Regular 'Skills and knowledge check' boxes will help you to keep on track with the knowledge and skills requirements for a unit. They will remind you to go back and refresh your knowledge if you haven't quite understood what you need to know or demonstrate. Tick off each one when you are confident you've nailed it.

> **Skills and knowledge check**
>
> ☐ I can describe the main stages of a risk assessment.
> ☐ I can identify what groups are protected by the Equality Act 2010.
> ☐ I can correctly and safely lift and carry boxes and heavy parcels.
> ☐ I understand the rights of consumers based on my knowledge of the Consumer Rights Act 2015.
>
> ○ I can list the eight rules or principles of data protection.
> ○ I know what is meant by COSHH.
> ○ I know what my main health and safety responsibilities at work are.
> ○ I know what the specific aspects of the Working Time Regulations are that refer to the working week.

What if…?

Employers need to know that you are responsible and that you understand the importance of what you are learning. These 'What if…?' scenarios will help you to understand the real links between theory and what happens in the workplace.

What if...?

You have organised an event and one of the attendees raises the alarm that a fire has been lit in the men's toilets. How would you handle this situation? Considerations should include:

1. remaining calm
2. calling emergency services
3. efficient and safe evacuation of participants
4. location of assembly points
5. checking that all participants are accounted for
6. reporting injuries.

Link it up

Although your BTEC Level 2 Technical is made up of several units, common themes are explored from different perspectives across the whole of your course. Everything you learn and do during your course will help you in your final assessment. This kind of assessment is called 'synoptic'. It means that you have the opportunity to apply all the knowledge and skills from the course to a practical, realistic work situation or task.

The 'Link it up' features show where information overlaps between units or within the same unit, helping you to see where key points might support your final assessment or help you gain a deeper understanding of a topic.

Step-by-step

This practical feature gives step-by-step descriptions of processes or tasks, and might include a photo or artwork to illustrate each step. This will help you to understand the key stages in the process and help you to practise the process or technique yourself.

Checklist

These lists present information in a way that is helpful, practical and interactive. You can check off the items listed to ensure you think about each one individually, as well as how they relate to the topic as a collective list.

Features connected to your assessment

Your course is made up of several units. There are two different types of unit:

- externally assessed
- internally assessed.

The features that support you in preparing for assessment are below. But first, what is the difference between these two different types of unit?

Externally assessed units

These units give you the opportunity to present what you have learned in the unit in a different way. They can be challenging, but will really give you the opportunity to demonstrate your knowledge and understanding, or your skills, in a direct way. For these units you will complete a task, set by Pearson, in controlled conditions. This could take the form of an exam or onscreen test, or it could be another type of task. You may have the opportunity to research and prepare notes around a topic in advance, which can be used when completing the assessment.

Link it up

Go to Unit 1 for more general information on the Data Protection Act 1998.

Internally assessed units

Internally assessed units involve you completing a series of assignments or tasks, set and marked by your tutor. The assignments you complete could allow you to demonstrate your learning in a number of different ways, such as a report, a presentation, a video recording or observation statements of you completing a practical task. Whatever the method, you will need to make sure you have clear evidence of what you have achieved and how you did it.

Ready for assessment

You will find these features in units that are internally assessed. They include suggestions about what you could practise or focus on to complete the assignment for the unit. They also explain how to gather evidence for assessment from the workplace or from other tasks you have completed.

> **Ready for assessment**
>
> Your office manager has asked you to provide cover for the receptionist, who will be on holiday for two weeks. You will be able to ask your colleagues and your office manager for guidance and assistance as you take on this role. You will be expected to work to the best of your ability on a daily basis.
>
> The receptionist has left notes to assist you with the tasks you will need to complete. You will have access to his manual desk diary and you also have access to your other colleagues' electronic diaries. Complete the following tasks.
>
> - Plan and prepare documentation for the next team meeting, including an agenda and an attendance list.
> - Create an itinerary for a colleague who is attending a business conference.
> - Design and prepare a leaflet for staff that identifies potential problems when using a photocopier and explain how to overcome them.
> - Produce a short presentation using appropriate software such as Microsoft PowerPoint®. A colleague has asked you to prepare six slides that she can use in a staff training session entitled 'Demonstrating positive personal behaviours'.

Assessment practice

These features include questions similar to the ones you'll find in your external assessment, so you can get some experience answering them. Each one relates to one or more Assessment Outcomes, as indicated in the top right-hand corner of this feature box. Suggested answers are provided at the end of Unit 1. Where 'Assessment practice' features require you to carry out your own research or give individual answers or opinions, however, no answers are provided.

Assessment practice — A01

A business administrator has to use all types of equipment.

Match the equipment to its main purpose. (2 marks)

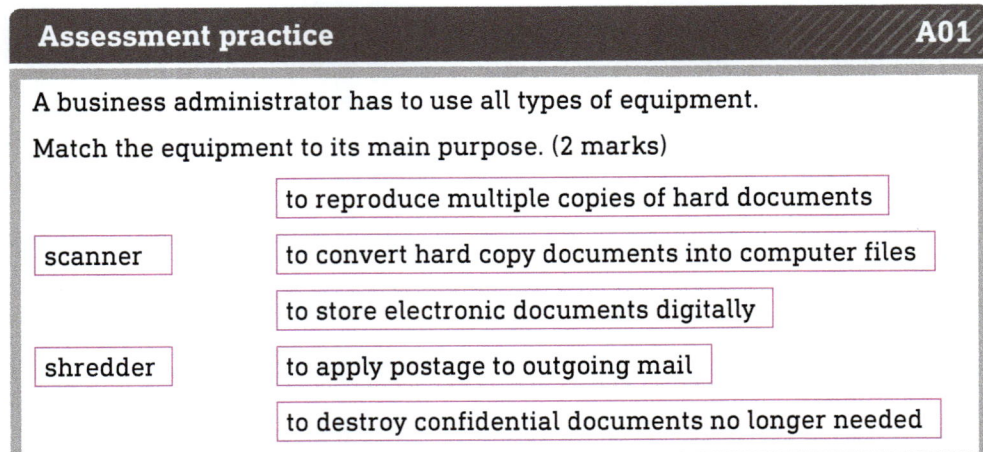

Getting ready for assessment

This section will help you prepare for external assessment. It gives information about what to expect in the final assessment, as well as revision tips and practical advice on preparing for and sitting exams or a set task. It provides a series of sample questions and answers that you might find, including helpful feedback, or 'verdicts', on the answers and how they could be improved.

Features which link your learning with the workplace

Work focus

Each unit ends with a 'Work focus' section, which links the learning from the unit to particular skills and behaviours that are required in the workplace. There are two parts in each 'Work focus' section:

1. **Hands on** – gives suggestions for tasks you could practise to develop the technical or professional skills you'll need on the job.
2. **Ready for work?** – supports you in developing the all-important transferable skills and behaviours that employers are looking for, such as adaptability, problem solving, communication or teamwork. It will give you pointers for showcasing your skills to a potential employer.

HANDS ON

There are some important technical and professional skills and competencies that you will need to practise which relate to this unit and your role as an administrator. Developing and practising these will help you make a good impression in your work experience as well as gaining employment in the future.

Using different types of office equipment

- For all the types of office equipment you use in your work experience, try to find the manuals and index them accordingly. Ensure that your colleagues know where they can be located and that they are accessible.

- Select two business-type photocopiers, either online or ones that you use or have used personally. Identify the brand name and key features and compare the two using an appropriate format, for example a table. Present this to your supervisor.

Use appropriate communication methods in a business or working environment

- Keep a log of any contact you have with customers or your tutor for one week and analyse the methods of communication you used. Say why each method was effective or, on reflection, whether another method should have been used.

Work effectively as part of a team

- For a work or social team, list all the members and identify the particular skills they bring to the team.

- Look for opportunities to support another team member in achieving a goal or target. Record your actions.

Understanding organisation structure

- Draw the organisational structure of your college, school or work placement, identifying the main levels and roles.

Ready for work?

Take this short quiz to find out whether you'd be the person chosen for that dream job.

1 When creating an event plan, you should:
- A record and prioritise preparation activities
- B get your workmate to write it
- C keep your plan in your head
- D not communicate your plan to others.

2 It is important to confirm roles and responsibilities to:
- A ignore instructions
- B understand what you have to do and when
- C get someone else to do it
- D know how not to do something.

3 Meeting minutes should be:
- A about how long the meeting will last
- B accurate records of meeting outcomes and actions
- C circulated three months after the event
- D not written at all.

4 When speaking to participants, you should:
- A chew gum
- B speak clearly and professionally
- C look up from your mobile phone
- D be rude and disrespectful.

5 If there is a fire at an event you should:
- A raise the alarm and evacuate the venue
- B go back and get your coat and bag
- C run like mad
- D put the fire out.

Your score:

If you scored mostly As, you may need to brush up on your event support skills. If you scored mostly Cs or Ds, go back and read the sections on planning, preparation and support. If you scored mostly Bs, you are ready for a role in event planning.

1 Understanding Administrative Services

Every organisation needs efficient administrative support and the role of an administrative assistant or practitioner is a vital and varied one. Whether you work in a small organisation or a larger company, you will need to know and understand a number of key tasks. These may include arranging travel and organising meetings; using office equipment; storing documents and managing mail services; working with and communicating with other people.

What skills do you think you need to work with others? Will you need to know about health and safety laws? What about the way the different parts of the organisation fit and work together? This unit will cover all these areas and more.

UNIT 1 | UNDERSTANDING ADMINISTRATIVE SERVICES

How will I be assessed?

By the end of the unit you will understand the different administrative roles and services. This includes providing administrative support for meetings and using different types of office equipment. You will also understand how different mail services work and become familiar with the arrangements for different types of business travel. Good working relationships are important in organisations, so you will learn about effective teamwork and good communication. There are many laws that affect organisations and as an administrative practitioner you will need to understand how they affect your role; this includes health and safety, the use of information and data, and equality in employment. You will also learn about the rights of consumers as well as the different types of business structure and ownership.

At the end of the unit you will be assessed using an onscreen test. The test contains both multiple choice and short answer questions.

Assessment outcomes

AO1 Demonstrate knowledge and recall of administrative services facts, key terms and definitions

AO2 Demonstrate understanding and application of administrative services and how working relationships contribute to an effective business

AO3 Be able to assess or analyse information, make connections for administrative services and the legal framework in which an organisation operates

AO4 Be able to assess or evaluate information on administrative services, suggesting/providing solutions, selecting and using appropriate evidence to support arguments and ideas from several sources, and providing arguments in familiar and unfamiliar contexts

What you will learn in this unit:

A   The different administrative roles and services

B   How working relationships contribute to an effective business

C   The legal framework in which your business operates

D   The structure in which the organisation operates

A The different administrative roles and services

As an administrator you will be asked to take on a number of roles and undertake many different tasks. It is very important that you understand how to carry out these roles and develop efficient planning skills in order to complete all tasks to a high standard.

A1 Providing administrative support for meetings

An important part of the role of an administrator is to plan, prepare, assist and support before, during and after meetings.

Meetings can be formal or informal. Informal meetings could be a group of people getting together to chat about a particular issue or problem. As an administrator you will primarily be asked to support formal meetings where specific procedures will have to be followed. Formal meetings typically include board management and team meetings.

Link it up

Go to Unit 4 to find out more about different types of meetings and events.

Practise

1. List three different types of formal meetings that are held in the organisation where you have a part-time job or work experience. Find out who attends the meetings and how often they are held.

2. Alternatively, talk to your tutor at school or college, or ask for permission to meet with a member of the administration team and ask them for three different examples of formal meetings they go to. Find out who attends these meetings.

There are several tasks that you will need to do no matter what the meeting type. These include some or all of the following.

Arranging and confirming date and time

First, find out and confirm who is attending the meeting. Sometimes there is already a list of who should attend. Next, get agreement on a date for the meeting. You might find that dates have already been set and put in staff diaries (some meetings are on the same day or date on a weekly or monthly basis). If not, suggest a number of potential dates and, from that list, choose the date when the maximum number of people can attend.

Booking a venue

If the meeting is located on the organisation's own premises, you may find rooms are already allocated as meeting rooms. Find out who is in charge of managing the diary or booking schedule for these rooms and ask for the agreed date to be confirmed. If the organisation is large with many rooms, it may have a computerised room booking system. If so, you should find out who has access to this system and ask them what rooms are free and whether they are suitable for the meeting. If a room is available, ensure it is booked for the meeting.

If the meeting is to be outside or external to the premises, you will need to look for companies that have meeting rooms or venues for hire, for example, large hotels. Each meeting will have its own **BUDGET**, which is the total amount of money allocated for a specific purpose. Check what the budget is for the meeting to ensure you do not spend more than is allocated.

Why is it important for the administrator to work closely with the chairperson or organiser prior to the start of the meeting?

Invite the attendees

You will need to send out an invite to everyone who is attending the meeting including the **CHAIRPERSON**. This is the person responsible for leading the meeting and ensuring it is conducted correctly. The invite needs to state the time, date and location. Normally, you will include a list of everyone attending the meeting. If there is to be an agenda (see Figure 1.1) the list of attendees will normally be included on this document.

Circulating agenda and required documents

The **AGENDA** is a schedule of items to be discussed at a meeting. It sets out the order of what is to be discussed. The first items are generally standard ones.

In addition, there may be a number of documents that need to be circulated before and at the meeting. If this is the case, you will need to collect these before the meeting from the relevant attendees, ensuring there are sufficient copies for everyone from the start of the meeting. Usually the agenda and associated documents are circulated via email or attached to the meeting invitation, so you need to ensure you have the email addresses of everyone who is attending, including anyone who is coming from outside the organisation.

Agenda Title

Date

Location

List of attendees including chairperson

List of documents to be circulated

1. Apologies for absence

2. Minutes of last meeting

3. Matters arising from the minutes

4. Agenda items

5. Any other business (AOB)

6. Date and time of next meeting.

Figure 1.1: Why is it important to agree on the agenda before a meeting? What would be the consequences of not doing this?

Arranging refreshments

You will need to arrange for some refreshments for everyone attending the meeting. Depending on the budget and the type of meeting, this could range from a sufficient supply of fresh water with water jugs and glasses/paper cups to a buffet meal if the meeting runs over lunchtime. The organisation may have the facilities to prepare its own food; if not, you will be required to source external catering suppliers.

Arranging equipment

Link it up

You will learn more about tools like Skype™ in Unit 3.

You should check with the attendees if they require any specific equipment for the meeting. This might include access to computers, internet access, overhead projectors, video equipment or any equipment required for attendees with special needs. Some attendees may be attending remotely, i.e. not in the room itself but using video conferencing tools such as Skype™.

Greeting attendees

If the meeting is located in the building, you might be required to meet attendees at reception and show them to the meeting room. You or the receptionist will need to ensure that attendees who are not employees of the organisation sign a visitors' file. This is for a number of reasons including health and safety. In addition, you may be required to provide attendees with visitor passes. The attendees should sign out and return their visitor passes before they leave the building.

Ensuring health and safety of attendees

Usually the chairperson will undertake this role and point out to attendees fire drill areas, emergency exits, the location of toilets and so on. You should confirm this information with the chairperson prior to the start of the meeting.

Practise

Investigate how you would accommodate participants with a disability when organising meetings at your workplace, including arrangements for wheelchair access, visual impairment and deafness.

Ensuring security of equipment and information

If equipment needed for the meeting is securely located elsewhere, find out who has access and ask their permission to move the equipment to the meeting room. Once the equipment is in the meeting room, keep the room locked when empty. Depending on the information that will be used in the meeting, you may need to comply with data protection regulations (covered later in this unit) and use only secure usernames and passwords for intranet access. Do not release these details to attendees who are not employees of the organisation. If attendees require only public access to the internet, your organisation may make this available through a 'guest' password.

Providing support during the meeting

Ask the chairperson if you are required to attend the meeting and, if so, where you will sit. You should confirm what your duties will be, for example, to be on hand to copy documents, communicate with technical support or ensure refreshments are always available.

Taking minutes, gaining approval and circulating

At all formal meetings it is necessary to take **MINUTES** of the meeting. These are an official record of the discussions and agreed actions from the meeting. As you become more experienced as an administrator you might be asked to take the minutes of the meetings you support.

You should proofread the minutes and then share them with the chairperson of the meeting. They will check the accuracy of the minutes and confirm that they are a true record of the meeting. You may need to amend the minutes after the chairperson has checked them. You will then be required to circulate the final, agreed minutes, generally by email. You should also attach any documents that were referred to in the meeting. The minutes are sent to all invitees, whether they attended the meeting or not.

> **Link it up**
>
> For more information on minutes go to Unit 4 and look at the section on taking and distributing minutes.

> **Practise**
>
> Ask your tutor if you can run a meeting with 8–10 of your fellow learners. This could be about issues with your course, your college or school or a forthcoming event. Alternatively, you could all take the role of employees to discuss typical work-related issues. Examples include organising a team-building event for the administration team; a change in the time that work starts from 9.00 a.m. to 8.30 a.m.; or the introduction of a new computerised room booking system.
>
> With your fellow learners, draw up an agenda, agree a chairperson, hold the meeting and write up a set of agreed minutes.

A2 Using different types of office equipment

As an administrator you will need to develop the skills to use a wide range of office equipment. Some may be specialised and specific to your role and the type of organisation you are working in, and some are used in most or all organisations. Some common types of equipment are discussed below.

> **Practise**
>
> In pairs, ask for permission to visit the administration areas or office of your school or college. List all the office equipment you can see, find out the purpose of each item of equipment and make a note of this.

Computer

All organisations use computers for some or all of their administrative needs. The computers may be desktop or laptop; laptop computers are more useful for staff who have to travel or move around the building. In most organisations, the computers will be connected to a network so that information and communication can be shared and sent via the intranet or email using the internal email address list.

You should expect to use a computer and the intranet for the following purposes:
- preparing documents, for example, using software applications to produce letters
- external and internal communication, for example, sending emails and distributing documents such as minutes of meetings
- electronic diary management for yourself and others
- storing documents
- making video or conference calls.

The factors to consider when using computers include:
- **safety**, for example, ergonomics and protection from spillages and live electricity connections
- **cost**, for example, costs of hardware and operating software
- **security**, for example, the use of passwords and usernames to protect personal information and data.

Printer

The purpose of a printer is to produce hard copies of the documents you have created on a computer. There are a number of factors an organisation will consider when choosing a printer. These include:
- volume (how much printing needs to be done)
- whether they need monochrome, black and white or colour printouts
- number of users
- print speed and printer memory (this affects the speed)
- resolution/quality and paper size
- size, especially if the printer will be located in a small office
- whether to choose an inkjet or laser jet printer – inkjets are usually smaller and slower than laser jet printers. However they are good for printing colour documents such as photographs. If used a lot, inkjet printers are relatively expensive to run because of the cost of cartridges. Laser jet printers are generally bigger and print more quickly. They are better for text documents as they produce a sharper image. They are also more efficient and cost effective if they will be used a lot.

Photocopier/scanner

Photocopiers are used to make copies of documents or images. A scanner, which can be separate or part of the photocopier, converts hard copy documents to computer files that can be stored electronically. Some scanners allow you to digitise the file so that it can be edited. There are a number of factors an organisation will consider when using a scanner or photocopier, as shown in Table 1.1.

UNIT 1 | UNDERSTANDING ADMINISTRATIVE SERVICES

Factor	Consideration
Cost	Photocopying many hard copy documents can be relatively expensive compared with scanning, storing and circulating scanned and digitised files.
Quality	Some photocopiers do not reproduce documents to a high quality; for example, the colour or definition of the copies will not reflect the originals.
Location	You may find the photocopier is not close to your work area.
Size	The photocopier may not have the paper capacity to print either the number of copies you need in one go or the size of the paper (e.g. A3, A5) you want to use.

Table 1.1: Factors to consider when using a photocopier or scanner

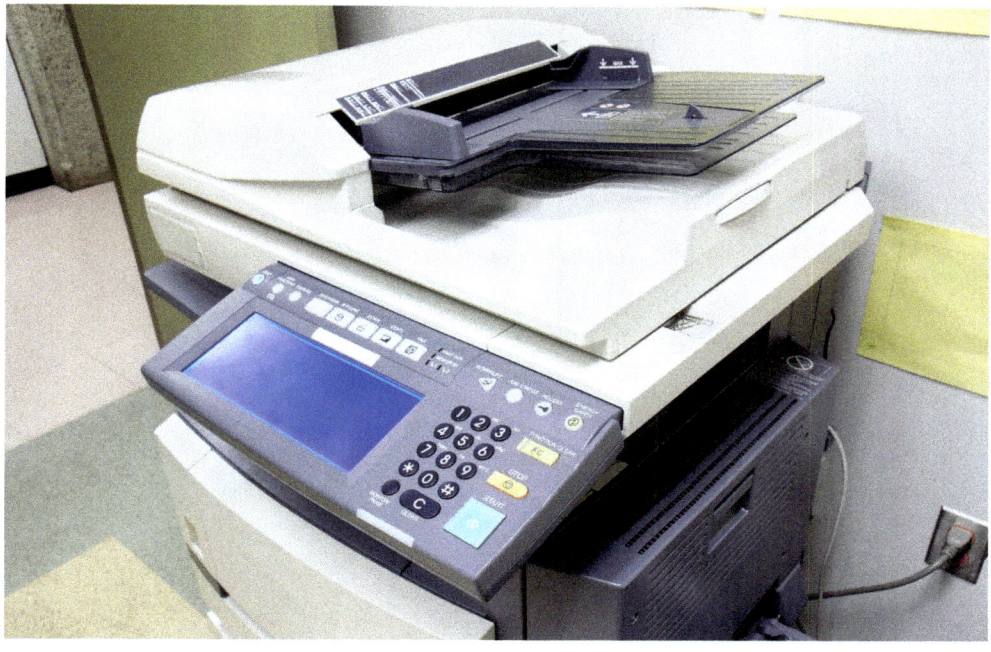

Can you think of situations where you would need to use a photocopier?

Telephone system

The basic purpose of a telephone system is to make and receive internal or external calls. The way in which calls are managed will depend on the type and size of the organisation. In large organisations, all calls go through a single, central telephone number to a specific person who will transfer the call via a screen to the appropriate person, department or office. In smaller organisations, calls could be picked up by any member of the team and transferred to the appropriate person. If that person is you, make sure you have a good understanding of who does what in the organisation.

Telephone features and functions that you may find useful include:
- **call transfer** – allows you to transfer a call to another member of staff (this can be done automatically on some systems)
- **conference call** – allows you to talk to several people at the same time
- **call waiting** – tells you if someone is trying to get through but cannot because you are already taking a call
- **secrecy button** – allows you to talk to a colleague without the caller being able to hear what is said
- **voicemail** – callers can leave a message if you are not able to pick up the phone or if the call is made outside office hours.

The functions and features you use will depend on your organisation, as shown in Table 1.2.

Table 1.2: Factors to consider when choosing a telephone system

Factor	Consideration
Volume of calls	In a big organisation, for example a large hotel, the telephone system will need to have all of the functions listed above and more. Otherwise, staff would not be able to handle the volume of calls to the business efficiently.
Use of mobile telephones	Many organisations provide some of their staff with mobile phones with their own designated number. This reduces the number of calls made through the main phone system and allows greater flexibility to make and answer calls at any time of the day, not just during office hours.
Cost	The more complicated the telephone system, the more costly it will be. Similarly, if a lot of employees use mobile phones, the cost of networks and new telephone sets may also be expensive. However, a cheaper, less reliable system might lead to customer complaints and frustration.

Why is it important to greet all telephone callers in a courteous and professional manner?

Practise

Find out what the specific telephone greetings are for the main telephone number and the department, team or personal telephone numbers in your college's student services department or your place of work. Practise these by recording yourself using your mobile phone and then listening back to the recordings.

Ask your tutor if you can send these recordings to them as an MP3 in order to get feedback on your performance.

Franking machine

A franking machine is used to print a marker on outgoing mail rather than attaching a postal stamp. A franking machine can be leased or purchased, which includes an upfront credit of postage, for example £20. One of your tasks may be to check the postage credit on the machine. It will need to be topped up before it reaches zero to ensure there is no delay in the posting of outward mail. You should also ensure that every piece of mail you send is individually franked and has not included the previous postage. Some aspects of using a franking machine are shown in Table 1.3.

Does your school or college use a franking machine?

Factor	Consideration
Cost	Discounts on the normal cost of postage are available through the use of a franking machine, although an initial value of postage has to be purchased upfront.
Location	The machine must be accessible for everyone who will be dealing with outgoing mail.
Size and functions	Modern franking machines can be linked to the internet, where the amount in the machine can be topped up online and images such as the company logo can be printed on the envelope.

Table 1.3: Factors to consider when using a franking machine

Shredder

The purpose of a shredder is to shred and destroy documents that are confidential and should not be available for others to see once they are no longer needed. There are different types of shredders including the ribbon cut shredder, which turns documents in to long strips; the cross cut, which produces small squares; and the diamond cut, which turns pages into small diamond-shaped pieces. The shredder an organisation chooses will depend on the factors shown in Table 1.4.

Table 1.4: Factors to consider when choosing a shredder

Factor	Consideration
Security	The most secure shredder is diamond cut. Ribbon or cross-cut shredded paper could be stuck back together to reproduce the original sheets easily.
Safety	Shredders have to be operated safely according to the instructions. Machines should have an auto stop in case the papers get jammed and thermal sensors to automatically turn off the machine if it overheats. All three types of shredder are equally suitable from this point of view.
Size	If you work for an organisation where there is a high volume of personal data, a bigger shredder will be needed to shred multiple sheets at one time. All three types of shredder are equally suitable from this point of view.
Location	The shredder should be located near where the original documents are stored to reduce the distance the documents need to be transported. The greater the distance, the more likely it is that others can see the data. All three types of shredder are equally suitable from this point of view.

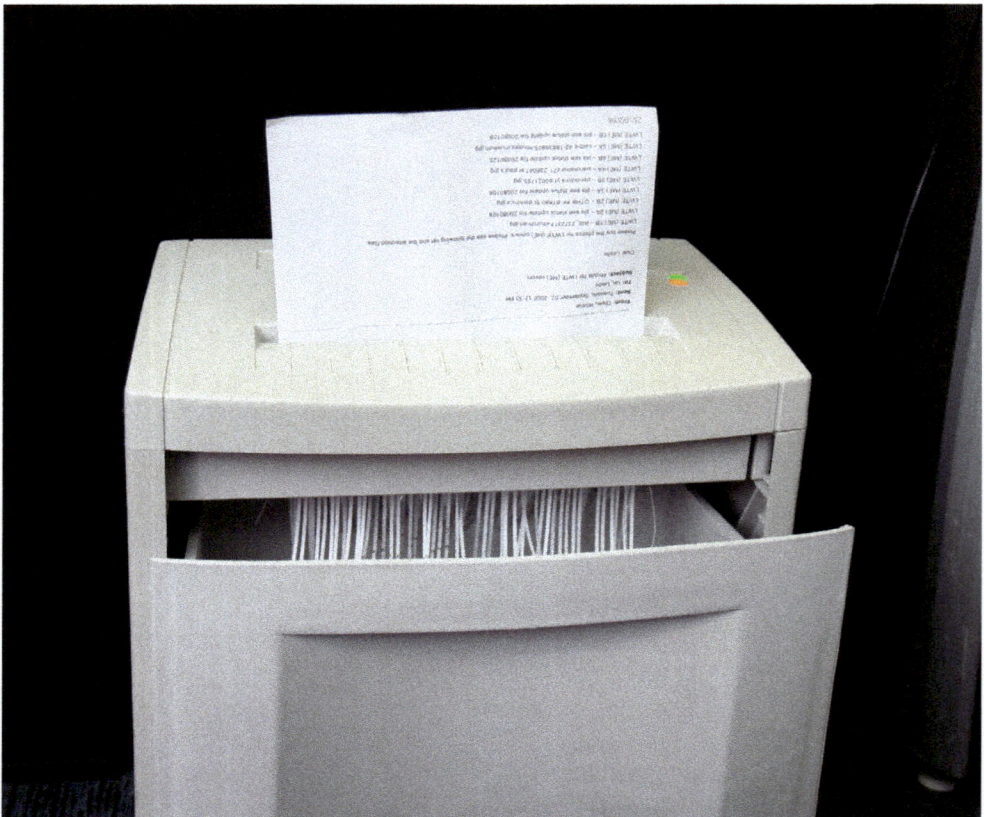

What kind of documents do you think should be shredded?

UNIT 1 | UNDERSTANDING ADMINISTRATIVE SERVICES

> **Assessment practice** — A01
>
> A business administrator has to use all types of equipment.
>
> Match the equipment to its main purpose. (2 marks)

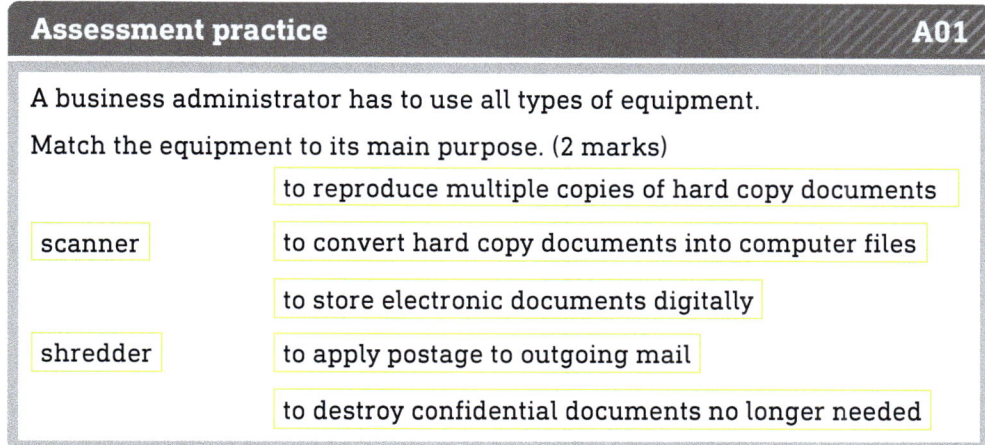

A3 Using different types of mail services

As an administrator you will deal with both incoming and outgoing mail. You need to understand the differences between the different mail services that are available to the organisation for outgoing mail and what the advantages and disadvantages are for these.

If the organisation you work for is small, you could be required to take the mail to a local post office or wait for a pickup. You may have to weigh and calculate the correct postage for letters and parcels.

Outgoing mail

There are a number of different mail services an organisation can use. Which one is chosen will depend on a number of factors:

- **urgency** – how quickly does the mail or parcel need to be with the addressee?
- **value** – is it a very valuable product that is being sent? This might also include a very important and confidential document.
- **insurance** – is the value of the letter or parcel high enough to need this?
- **proof of delivery** – do you want a record of when and by whom the mail or parcel was received?
- **location** – where is the addressee? Are they local or in another country?

All the above factors will affect how much the mail will cost. You may need to discuss with your supervisor which option to take before going ahead with the despatch.

The services available for you to choose from are:

- **first-class letter mail** – mail will be delivered by the next working day. This is more expensive than second-class letter mail.
- **second-class letter mail** – mail will be delivered within three working days. The cost of postage will be determined by the size and weight of the mail for both first- and second-class mail.
- **international mail** – if the addressee is overseas you will have to use international mail services. This means either:
  - **airmail** – all letters to Europe are sent this way, as well as small parcels up to 2 kg and pamphlets up to 5 kg
  - **surface mail** – this mail is delivered by road, rail and ship and tends to be used for larger deliveries that cannot be sent by airmail. This is slower than airmail.
- **special delivery** – this service guarantees next day delivery by a particular time, such as 9.00 a.m. or 1.00 p.m. The sender will receive compensation if that guarantee is not met. This service is more expensive than first or second-class mail.

- **recorded delivery** – the receiver of the mail or parcel has to sign as proof of delivery. Appropriate documentation has to be completed by the despatching post office or by the organisation sending the mail.
- **courier services** – if there is a very urgent need to send a letter or parcel to someone, you can hire a courier to collect the mail immediately and deliver it directly to the addressee. This is often used by businesses within the same city, but can also be regional or national. This service is expensive compared to first and second-class mail. Couriers should have goods in transit insurance. Some transporters may also have additional levels of insurance cover. Transport providers are required to state their level of insurance cover on their profiles or company details; you should check this is sufficient to cover the cost of replacement of the goods being transported.

Research what letter and parcel options the Royal Mail offers with regard to size and weight

Practise

Find out what postal services are best for sending a 2.5 kg parcel from Leeds to an address in Glasgow. The parcel has to be there within 24 hours.

Internal mail

This type of mail is sent from one member of staff to another. You might need to take this directly to the individual concerned. In larger organisations, there will be a mail room where each person, team or department has their own **PIGEONHOLE**, which is a space where all the mail for a particular location is placed, often in the form of a storage unit made up of square boxes; each box has a staff member's name on it and holds their mail and/or documents. You or another administrator may need to collect the mail and distribute it accordingly. Alternatively, the organisation may have staff whose job it is to handle all the mail and deliver it according to set procedures and times.

You may need to deal with **ENCLOSURES** (items enclosed with the main document or letter). You need to ensure that these items are securely attached to the main document and not left in the envelope when distributed. Some documents may be confidential, for example employee or customer information. You must ensure that this mail is passed safely and securely to its intended recipient. You should not **DISCLOSE** (reveal secret or confidential information) anything you may have read or seen, neither should you open any confidential document if you do not need to. You may also be required to 'date stamp' incoming mail; this is to provide evidence that you have received the mail.

A4 Arranging business travel

As part of your role as an administrator, you could be tasked with arranging business travel for others in your organisation, particularly managers. To do this effectively you need to be familiar with the options available to you. You must also know what to do if problems arise.

In the first instance, find out what the organisation's procedures are for booking tickets; for example does the company use a general travel agent, a specialist booking agent or book tickets directly online?

Arrangements

There are a number of things you need to confirm when making travel arrangements:
- final destination address
- the number and names of the people travelling
- dates of travel
- preferred travel times
- preferred type of travel (see page 16)
- budget – confirm with your manager, or the people travelling, how much you have to spend as this will be a big influence on which type of travel you book
- departure and destination points – depending on the mode of transport, the departure point could be an airport, railway station or ferry port. You may need to arrange further transport to and from these points for individuals travelling. You should try and make these points as convenient as possible for the travellers
- passport, VISA and insurance requirements – if the travel is to another country, you should check what documentation the travellers need. If going to Paris, for example, they will need a current passport. If going outside the European Union, for example to China, they will require a visa, which is an official document that allows a named person to enter, travel through and leave a specified country. You will also need to check if the organisation already has suitable insurance to meet the needs of the travellers. If not, you may need to get extra insurance through the organisation's insurance broker
- preparing and supplying a travel ITINERARY – this is a travel plan and timetable of activities for a member of staff who is going away on a business trip. It will usually include the following details:
  - methods of transport, destination and departure points
  - detailed travel times, for example travel and pickup times, departure and arrival times
  - hotel
  - car rental if required
  - day schedules, for example meeting times, contact names
  - supply of all documentation, for example tickets, visas, itineraries, insurance certificates
- accurate records – you will need to keep records of all travel and hotel documents in order to account for all the costs incurred and to balance these against the allocated budget and any expenses the travellers claim.

Types of travel

There are different forms of transport that you can choose. Each one will have different pricing and booking procedures. Your decision will depend on a number of factors including price, distance, reliability, suitability and urgency. Your organisation might also have a preferred option depending on their environmental policy.

Consider a request to arrange travel to Paris in France. To get to Paris you could use any or a number of the methods shown in Table 1.5.

Table 1.5: Different ways to travel to Paris

Mode of transport	Direct/indirect travel	Considerations
Air	Flights go direct from the UK to Paris.	There are different standards or classes of air travel: • Economy – this is the cheapest type with few added extras. You may get free tea, coffee and soft drinks together with snacks. • Business – this is a more expensive travel choice and will include better seating, more legroom, meals and access to passenger lounges at airports.
Train	Trains go direct to Paris, first using a normal train service to get to London and then taking the Eurostar direct to Paris.	National train services include: • Standard class – these are the cheapest types of seats. You can make reservations and may be able to get discounts depending on the time of travel and whether you have a day ticket or season ticket. • First class – these are more expensive tickets that offer better seats, worktables, free drinks and Wi-Fi access. • Eurostar – this train service goes from St Pancras in London direct to Paris via the Channel Tunnel.
Ferry	Ships depart from many ports in the UK to a number of ports in France.	It is possible to take a car on the ferry and so this may be more economical when a number of people are in the travelling party. Your party will then travel by car from the port in France to Paris. It is also possible to be a 'foot passenger' on a ferry. You would then need to arrange further travel arrangements at the port to get the party to Paris.
Car	It is possible to drive all the way to Paris via Eurotunnel.	Depending on your organisation's policy, you will have to find out what vehicles are available to use. The options could include: • the employee's personal vehicle • a hire car from a rental company • a 'pool' car if your organisation has its own vehicles that are available for employees to use • taxis to get the employee to the departure point and from the destination point to the final address.

How long does it take to get from London to Paris on the Eurostar?

UNIT 1 | UNDERSTANDING ADMINISTRATIVE SERVICES

Problems and their impact

You should be prepared for problems to arise at any stage of the process. If problems are not properly managed or **CONTINGENCIES** (plans for possible future events) put in place, a number of negative consequences could occur. For example, the reputation of the organisation could be harmed if the travellers fail to turn up at an important meeting. Your own reputation will also be affected if you have not put together a properly structured itinerary or have forgotten to include important documents. The organisation may then miss important business opportunities and lose income if the travel arrangements do not get the right people to the right place at the right time. Finally, if the travel arrangements do not go as planned and do not have the expected outcomes, time and money will have been wasted.

Problems can arise because of:
- **unclear communication** – the traveller wants to travel from their local train station rather than a mainline and a wrong ticket is booked
- **delays and cancellations** – if there is bad weather on the day of travel, alternative arrangements may have to be made urgently
- **accidents** – if travelling by road, accidents can severely disrupt travel arrangements. Additional time should be built into your itineraries to allow for such occurrences
- **lack of resources** – the preferred type of travel may not be possible based on the budget or resources that are available. You will then need to provide the traveller with affordable options for them to make a choice
- **important documents out of date** – passports, visas or insurance could be out of date and prevent travel abroad.

> **Practise**
>
> Investigate the travel options, including costs, of travelling from Manchester to a business exhibition at a large arena in London. The exhibition is midweek. There will be two travellers, one senior manager and one assistant manager, and they will need overnight accommodation for one night.

A5 Storing business documents

It is important to understand how to correctly store, secure and protect business documents, whether they are paper documents or digital files.

The reasons for this are:
- the legal responsibilities of the organisation
- the financial cost of storing large amounts of business documents, particularly paper documents
- the constant need to refer to past documents and records , and retrieve them easily
- the need to use digital and physical storage space efficiently.

17

Security and confidentiality

The Data Protection Act lays down specific constraints on the use of personal data by organisations. This is covered in more detail in later units; however it is necessary to consider all business documents, personal and otherwise, when deciding how they should be secured and, where necessary, how to restrict access to confidential personal and business documents.

Access to electronic or digital media can be restricted through the use of usernames and passwords. The organisation can also decide which users have access to which documents. In addition, different servers can be used to store different types of documents with added security on some servers. Other online data storage services can also be used to store and share less confidential documents.

All organisations will have procedures to **BACK UP** (securely store and/or restore) electronic data. In large organisations, this will be one process across all the organisation's servers and will be overseen by trained technicians. In smaller organisations, one individual may be responsible for backing up the day's transactions on a CD or similar type of storage. Individually, you should always ensure you save your work on a regular basis, either to your PC or on a memory stick. Make sure you follow any data protection rules that apply.

The types of documents that need to be stored securely include:

- **personnel records** – job applications, sickness records, disciplinary records, appraisal records
- **financial records** – income tax (PAYE) and value added tax (VAT), records, invoices, expense claims, banking documents
- **health and safety records** – risk assessments, insurance certificates, accident reports
- **customer records** – payment records, addresses, personal data of individual customers.

Businesses are required by law to keep certain documents, particularly financial ones, for a particular length of time; these include PAYE and VAT records. You should check with your supervisor what policies are currently in place. Documents should be clearly marked with a start and end date to show how long they should be stored.

Paper documents

Physical access to paper or hard copy documents can be restricted simply by ensuring that drawers and filing cabinets are locked as well as the rooms in which they are located. Cabinets need to be large enough and in sufficient numbers to house all the documents to be stored.

Any storage system should be organised so that required documents can be located and accessed easily. In order to do this, organisations use various methods of indexing or organising their files. Examples of these methods are shown in Table 1.6.

UNIT 1 | UNDERSTANDING ADMINISTRATIVE SERVICES

Filing method	Definition
Numerical	This system uses a sequential numerical reference, for example 1.1, 1.2, 1.3. The advantages of this are simplicity, ease of access and that each document is given a unique reference. The scale of the index is infinite and only limited by the physical or digital storage capacity available.
Chronological	This system stores and references documents in date order. A subcategory, for example alphabetical customer surname, will normally be used in addition to this system.
Alphabetical	This system files documents using the letters A–Z. This could be by surname, company name or product. A disadvantage of this might be where there are similar names, for example surnames like Smith; however, in the event of this the first name will be used as a secondary index. The advantage of this system is its ease of use for searching and access.
Alphanumerical	This system uses a mix of letters and numbers. An example might be room numbers in a school or college: for example room B22 would be room number 22 on the B corridor.

Table 1.6: Methods for organ sing paper documents

Electronic documents

There should always be a back up procedure in place for electronic storage systems. This is usually managed by technical staff in the organisation at the end of each day's activities, and may involve transferring data to a different server, hard drive or CD. As an individual you should also back up personal work regularly but check first if there are particular organisation protocols or procedures that need to be followed for legal reasons.

All backed-up data should be password protected, whether it is information and data you have used in your own role or for the organisation as a whole. You should always ensure any passwords you use are kept secure and are a mix of numbers, letters and symbols.

> **Link it up**
>
> Go to Unit 3 to find out more on how to use business technology to store business documents safely and securely.

Skills and knowledge check

☐ I can list the different types of mail service available to organisations from the cheapest to the most expensive.
☐ I can explore different ways of travelling to find the best option for a business trip.
☐ I can overcome potential problems during business travel through planning and preparation.
☐ I can index paper-based documents using different methods.

○ As an administrator I know how to prepare for a meeting.
○ I know how to structure an agenda.
○ I know how to use the different types of equipment and machines found in a business environment.
○ I know what kinds of documents need to be stored securely in an organisation and why.

B How working relationships contribute to an effective business

For an administrator, knowing and understanding the principles and practices of effective teamwork in a business environment is important. In this section, you will learn about the crucial skills you need to develop to become an effective member of a team.

B1 Communication

COMMUNICATION is defined as the sending of information from one person or group to another person or group, for a given purpose. There are three basic stages to all types of communication, as shown in Figure 1.2.

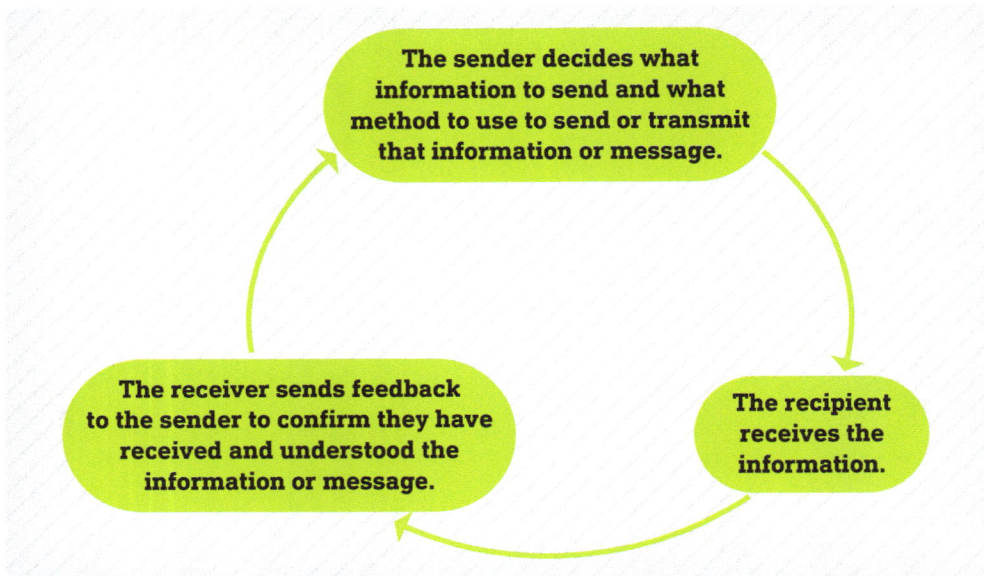

Figure 1.2: The three basic stages of communication

Good communication is vital in any organisation. As an administrator, you must have good communication skills. You role will involve communicating with many different people; knowing how to do this effectively is vital in developing good working relationships and an effective team.

There are three main methods of communication: verbal, non-verbal and written.

Verbal communication skills

Verbal communication can be formal (for example in meetings) or informal (for example a chat over coffee in the canteen). **FACE-TO-FACE** discussions (talking to someone in person) or using a telephone are the most common forms of verbal communication. Other examples include presentations, attending meetings and using video conferencing tools such as Skype™.

When communicating with others, the style of language you use is important. You should speak clearly and properly. Try not to speak too quickly in meetings and presentations. You should consider the culture and background of the person you are talking to and their level of understanding.

When talking to others, be aware of your **TONE OF VOICE**, which includes the volume, pitch and quality of the voice. Do you sound angry or disinterested? You should be courteous and respectful at all times.

Practise

Say the following to another learner in the class: 'Good morning, MBV Transport Services, (insert your name) speaking, how can I help you today?' first with a smile on your face and then with an angry face. How did this make you feel? How did your fellow learner react?

In your role as an administrator you should have confidence in yourself and in what you are saying. You should ensure that you are well prepared and you know the purpose of the communication and the needs of your audience. Depending on the type of organisation, you may be required to look smart and businesslike; this will give others more confidence in you and what you are saying than if you look untidy and less businesslike.

You should always respond appropriately to others. This might be formal, for example to customers and senior managers, or informal when talking to your colleagues and team. If you are on reception or answering the telephone there may be a formal, agreed way of responding to others. When responding to your colleagues, be polite and respectful at all times. Listen carefully to what they are saying or asking and request clarification if you are not sure. You will then be able to respond in the right way.

Written communication skills

In any organisation you will need good written communication skills when preparing emails, letters, agendas, minutes of meetings, notices or reports. You will also need good written communication skills if you are required to use social media as part of your job role.

With any written communication you must be clear what you are writing about – in other words the content of your communication. You must explain exactly what you want people to know or do, for example to attend a meeting at a given time, date and place.

Your communication should be **ACCURATE** (correct and precise), particularly if you are including numerical information, for example getting a decimal point in the right place. Always double check you have the correct information and you are passing this on accurately. Do not try to change or reword the message.

You should not add content or lengthen the communication for the sake of it; your communication should be concise and to the point with no unnecessary words or paragraphs. A good rule of thumb is that a sentence should not be more than 30 words and a paragraph no more than ten lines. Any routine business communication should have a limited number of paragraphs – three or four is probably sufficient.

Link it up

Go to Unit 2 to learn more about written communications in different work situations. This will be important when you attempt a synoptic assessment.

Always use plain English and everyday words in a friendly but direct style. Do not use **SLANG** – informal language and words that are not appropriate for formal communications. How direct and formal you are will depend on the purpose of the communication and who you are writing to. There may be guidelines, rules and procedures you have to follow. Always check with your line manager; for example you may need to use a particular style and size of font in written communication.

Visit the Plain English Campaign website and read the guidance on how to improve your own written communication

Another good habit to adopt is to always check your communication before you send it. This is particularly important with emails as poorly written communication can be misinterpreted (see Figure 1.3). Once you have pressed 'send', an email cannot be retrieved.

Figure 1.3: Can you list five words that sound the same but are spelled differently, and explain their meanings?

Punctuation, spelling and grammar are very important in the business environment. It is good practice to check that you have spelled words correctly; otherwise you may give a poor impression to the recipient of the communication, both of yourself and the organisation. Remember, computer spellcheckers often use American English rather than UK English. As a result, they may show that a word is spelled incorrectly when it is not and vice versa. Change the settings on your computer if you can.

UNIT 1 | UNDERSTANDING ADMINISTRATIVE SERVICES

Non-verbal communication skills

Non-verbal communication (NVC) is what you communicate to others without actually saying or writing anything. It can be as effective as speech or writing in getting a message across. There are many examples of NVC, all of which might be observed in a single meeting or presentation to a group of people.

A person's face is the most obvious source of outward expression, and can show very clearly how they feel: a smile compared with a frown, for example. Eye contact can also suggest how someone feels about what they are being told. In a meeting, making eye contact can suggest someone is interested in what you're saying and is paying attention. Avoiding eye contact and looking into the distance could suggest someone is uninterested or withholding information from you or others.

Your **BODY LANGUAGE** can also communicate some kind of meaning. This is a physical, non-verbal form of communication in which your body position or gestures convey some feeling or intention. Common examples are waving goodbye or shaking someone's hand. Standing too close to someone can be intimidating and should be avoided. In addition there are cultural differences that should be considered with regard to touch, clothing and methods of introduction.

> **Practise**
>
> In groups, using only body language (no words or written communication) communicate the following information or messages.
>
> 1. Imagine the group is a work team. You are their manager and you are happy with how they have performed in the last week.
> 2. Imagine the group is talking about something not relevant to a task at hand. You are getting restless and want to get back to work.
> 3. There is one particular member of the group you want to keep your distance from for personal reasons.

If someone's body position or posture is leaning forward in a meeting, this suggests they are interested in what you are talking about and may be willing to contribute to the discussion. In contrast, leaning backwards with folded arms might suggest someone is indifferent or doesn't agree with what is being discussed.

Investigate what skills are needed by the chairperson of a meeting to ensure all attendees make a valuable contribution

Finally, active listening is another important NVC skill you should try to develop. You can show you are actively listening by making good eye contact with the other person. This gives the impression you are interested in what they are saying and you want to understand exactly what it is they are trying to tell you. You can also show your interest by clarifying what you think they mean, responding appropriately using NVC or suggesting they tell you more.

Impact of poor communication

Good communication skills are very important as poor communication can have a negative impact on you and the organisation. Some of these negative impacts are listed below.

- **Misunderstandings** – there are many potential examples of misunderstandings that can arise as a result of poor communication. If a meeting invitation is sent out with the wrong meeting time, colleagues and any external invitees will turn up at the wrong time. They will be upset and their whole working day may have been wasted.
- **Poor relationships with other staff** – if some staff receive less accurate and clear information than others about important changes in the organisation, they may feel they have been treated unfairly or they may worry that there is bad news ahead.
- **Mistakes** – if you do not check what you have said or written is accurate, for example financial or numerical information, then ongoing plans will be based on incorrect assumptions.
- **Missed deadlines** – if you are asked to take minutes or notes for a meeting, you must record this information accurately. For example, if you write down the wrong deadlines, whole projects could fail because people will not complete their work in time.
- **Complaints** – if you are working on reception and you greet someone in a disrespectful way, for example with incorrect body language or the wrong name, then the customer or client may complain to your line manager because you were not businesslike.

B2 Teamwork

All organisations and businesses are made up of many different teams. Sometimes there will be smaller teams within big teams; for example the department you work in is a team, but you may well be part of an administration team within that department.

Putting employees into teams has many benefits for an organisation including the following.

- A greater variety of issues and problems can be tackled by bringing together more expertise.
- Staff working together boosts morale as employees gain support from each other.
- Opportunities for improvements that cross different teams and departments can be found more easily.
- Recommendations that come from the team itself are more likely to be implemented than if they come from just one person or a manager.

A happy and effective team will work together to solve problems and achieve targets

Members of a team will have well-defined job roles but there may still be friction between the different personalities of individuals. This can largely be avoided by understanding and valuing people's differences and ensuring that you and others in the team develop the skills required to be good team members.

Skills and requirements of working as a team

Organisations look to develop the following skills in good team members.

Cooperation

It is important that you put the team's targets before your own. You will be expected to look at the 'whole picture' and incorporate ideas and solutions that are best for the team, over and above your own.

Learning from others

Always take the opportunity to learn from others in the team. You could ask to meet with others in similar roles to talk about how they do their jobs. You could also ask to shadow someone doing a similar or more senior role to see how other teams work.

Meeting agreed deadlines

You will be expected to be motivated to achieve your set targets and goals and do whatever is necessary to meet them.

Achieving quality standards

As a team member you should find out what standards, benchmarks or deadlines the team is working towards. You will then need to find out how you can contribute to achieving these targets. This might involve setting your own personal benchmarks and monitoring yourself to ensure you are on target.

Positive attitude

Every team member should be able to trust and rely on every other team member. This positive attitude will be crucial in developing excellent relationships with your colleagues.

Willingness

You should be prepared to take on any jobs and tasks allocated to you, not just the ones you would like to do.

Showing support

You will be expected to be willing to help other team members, for example if they are struggling to meet a deadline.

Accepting others' strengths and weaknesses

One of the most important skills you need to develop is to accept that each person in the team is different. They will come from different backgrounds with a variety of experience, points of view, skills and opinions. Every person in the team will need support from you and your colleagues to build on their strengths and improve on their weaknesses.

Acknowledging your own strengths and weaknesses

You will be asked to build on your strengths and improve on your weaknesses by, for example, looking for opportunities to develop these areas. Opportunities to improve include shadowing other administrators to see how they do their job or taking more formal training.

Receiving and offering feedback

All team members need to know what they are doing well and not so well. As a team member you will be given formal feedback (an appraisal) from your team leader or manager at set dates and periods throughout the year. You may also be given informal feedback by the team leader or other team members throughout the year. You should accept constructive criticism positively and look to improve on any areas of weakness. Any feedback should be given in private, particularly if it is negative.

Displaying courteous behaviour

You will be expected to accommodate the reasonable demands made on you by the team in a polite and professional manner at all times. This might include meeting deadlines, following set procedures, attending meetings, and responding in a timely and polite manner to emails and telephone calls.

Teamwork in the workplace allows the organisation and staff to become more familiar with each other and to learn how to work together in more productive and effective ways.

>
> **Link it up**
>
> Go to Unit 2 to learn more about demonstrating professional behaviour in a workplace.

Results of working as an effective team

Good teamwork has many benefits for the organisation and will contribute to its success.

Provision of quality goods and services

A team working together, sharing ideas and supporting each other can continuously improve the goods and services the business produces or provides.

Good reputation for self

By supporting the team and the individuals within it, and acting professionally at all times, you will develop a good reputation as someone who is reliable and good in their role as an administrator.

Self-development

You will improve your knowledge and skills by working with a good team who are happy to share their knowledge and experience with you.

Job satisfaction

You are happy at work and feel as though you are doing an interesting and worthwhile job in a supportive working atmosphere.

Reputation of organisation

As the quality of goods and services improves, and staff become better at what they do, customers will want to buy more from the organisation and people will want to join it as employees.

Maintained or increased business

With an improved reputation and reliable employees, the organisation will please its clients and not lose them to other organisations. In addition, more business will be gained from current and new customers who have heard about the good reputation of the organisation.

Financial security

With improved levels of business the organisation can expect to maintain high levels of sales which will lead to fewer worries about paying wages and costs.

Assessment practice — A02

Explain one skill that organisations look to develop in good team members. (2 marks)

Skills and knowledge check

- ☐ I can describe the key differences between verbal and non-verbal communication.
- ☐ I can identify and explain the difference between tone and content of written communication.
- ☐ I can practise active listening.
- ☐ I can identify the three stages of communication.

- ○ I know how my body language can influence what others think of my performance at work.
- ○ I know how to respond to customer enquiries.
- ○ I know what skills I need to develop to become a good and effective team member.
- ○ I understand the benefits of effective working teams.

C The legal framework in which your business operates

All organisations are legally bound by many different laws and regulations. Your organisation may have specialists who are experts in particular areas, or it may hire people who are, such as solicitors. As an administrator you are not expected to advise other staff on these laws, but you do need to have a general awareness of the regulations and the ways in which they affect you and your colleagues.

C1 Use and storage of information

All organisations are bound by the Data Protection Act 1998 in the storage, use and handling of personal information and data.

The Data Protection Act 1998 sets out eight rules or 'principles' governing the use of personal information. All organisations must comply with these principles, unless an exemption applies. The principles are in essence a code of good practice for processing personal data.

1. **First principle** – personal data must be processed fairly and lawfully.
2. **Second principle** – personal data can only be obtained for specified and lawful purposes, and cannot be used for any other purpose. The person has to be told what that purpose is.
3. **Third principle** – personal data should be 'adequate, relevant and not excessive'. The organisation should only hold the minimum amount of information they need for a particular purpose.
4. **Fourth principle** – personal data should be accurate and kept up to date. People have the right to see what data is held on them and can request data to be corrected if it is not accurate.
5. **Fifth principle** – personal data cannot be kept for longer than is necessary.
6. **Sixth principle** – personal data must be processed in accordance with the rights of the person whose data it is, such as confidentiality and their human rights.
7. **Seventh principle** – secure and appropriate technical and organisational procedures should be in place to prevent unauthorised or unlawful processing of personal data and to stop accidental loss or destruction of the data.
8. **Eighth principle** – personal data cannot be transferred to a country or territory outside the European Union, unless that country or territory has an adequate level of protection for the rights and freedoms of individuals in relation to the processing of personal data.

As an administrator you should be aware of these principles and the procedures your organisation has in place to ensure these principles are enforced.

UNIT 1 | UNDERSTANDING ADMINISTRATIVE SERVICES

> **Practise**
>
> Discuss with other learners what type of information 'personal data' might include.

> **Practise**
>
> Your fellow administrator has been asked to type up some letters by a particular deadline, so they copy some personal data onto a memory stick to finish the letters at home. Which of the rules set out by the Data Protection Act 1998 has been broken and why?

C2 Employers' and employees' responsibilities under health and safety legislation

Every organisation has a responsibility to ensure it follows the relevant rules and regulations with regard to the health, safety and wellbeing of its employees. Equally, as an employee, you have your own responsibilities to uphold. This section explains the essential rights and responsibilities for every employee and employer that, as an administrator, you should understand.

The main law governing health and safety at work in the United Kingdom is the Health and Safety at Work Act 1974 (HASAWA). This states that all organisations must do what is reasonably practicable to ensure high standards of health and safety.

In summary it is the organisation's responsibility to provide:

- a safe place of work
- a safe system of work
- adequate plant and equipment
- competent and safety-conscious staff
- information that is easy to understand and follow so workers are aware of the hazards and risks they face, the measures in place to control the risks, and how to follow any emergency procedures
- procedures and clear instructions
- adequate health and safety training that is relevant and effective; this should take place during work hours and must be provided free of charge
- an appropriate level of supervision, particularly for new, inexperienced and young workers
- monitoring and surveillance of all aspects of health and safety
- plans for emergencies.

It is your responsibility as an employee to:

- take care of your own health and safety and that of others by ensuring you work in a safe and sensible way at all times
- co-operate with your employer and your colleagues with regard to health, safety and wellbeing at work
- adhere to the safe working practices the organisation has implemented, for example fire evacuation drills and manual handling procedures
- report to your manager any potential hazards
- not use safety equipment incorrectly or maliciously, such as fire extinguishers.

The maintenance of a healthy and safe working environment

As part of managing health and safety your organisation must control the risks in the workplace. To do this, managers need to think about what might cause harm to people and decide whether the organisation is taking reasonable steps to prevent that harm. This process of assessing the likelihood and seriousness of certain hazards in the workplace is known as **risk assessment**, and it is something the organisation is required by law to carry out. (If the organisation has fewer than five employees it does not have to write anything down but still needs to do the assessment.) A risk assessment is not about creating huge amounts of paperwork but rather about identifying sensible measures to control risk in the workplace. The stages are shown in Figure 1.4.

Identify the hazards
One of the most important aspects of risk assessment is accurately identifying the potential hazards in your workplace.

Decide who might be harmed
The organisation has to consider how employees (or others who may be present, such as contractors or visitors) might be harmed. This will help to identify the best way of controlling the risk. That doesn't mean listing everyone by name, but rather identifying groups of people (for example, 'people working in the storeroom' or 'passers-by').

Evaluate the risks
Having identified the hazards, the organisation must assess how likely it is that harm will occur and the level of risk and decide what to do about it. Risk is a part of everyday life and the organisation is not expected to eliminate all risks. Instead, they must make sure all the main risks, and the things to be done to manage them responsibly, are known. Generally, everything reasonably practicable should be done to protect people from harm. The organisation is not expected to anticipate unforeseeable risks.

Record your findings
Records of significant findings are made. This includes the hazards, how they might harm people and what is in place to control the risks. Any record produced should be simple and focused on controls.

Figure 1.4: Identifying sensible measures to control risk in the workplace

Practise

While on your work experience ask your manager if you can see a risk assessment. Does it follow all the stages indicated above? Can you add anything to it?

Alternatively, ask for permission to view all of your teaching rooms. What can you see that might be a risk to health and safety? What control methods are in place? Are they sufficient? Discuss your findings with your tutor.

UNIT 1 | UNDERSTANDING ADMINISTRATIVE SERVICES

Reporting of Injuries, Diseases and Dangerous Occurrences Regulations (RIDDOR) 2013

This law requires employers (or, in certain circumstances, others who control or manage the premises) to report to the relevant enforcing authority and keep records of:
- work-related deaths
- work-related accidents which cause certain specified serious injuries to workers, or which result in a worker being incapacitated for more than seven consecutive days
- cases of those industrial diseases listed in RIDDOR
- certain 'dangerous occurrences' (near-miss accidents)
- injuries to a person who is not at work, such as a member of the public, which are caused by an accident at work and which result in the person being taken to hospital from the site for treatment.

Personal protective equipment

Employers have certain responsibilities relating to the supply and use of personal protective equipment (PPE) at work. PPE is equipment that protects the employee or member of the public against health or safety risks at work. It can include items such as safety helmets, gloves, eye protection, high-visibility clothing, safety footwear and safety harnesses. It also includes respiratory protective equipment. It is unlikely you will need such equipment in a business or office environment unless, for example, you are asked to visit an area where there is construction work.

> **Practise**
>
> At your college or school, find as many different fire extinguishers as you can. Note what kind of fire they can be used for and the date they were checked.

It is a duty of the employer to provide all necessary protective equipment and clothing

Safe manual handling

The term manual handling covers a wide variety of activities including lifting, lowering, pushing, pulling and carrying. If any of these tasks are not carried out appropriately there is a risk of injury.

Manual handling causes over a third of all workplace injuries, including work-related musculoskeletal disorders (MSDs) such as pain and injuries to arms, legs and joints, and repetitive strain injuries. To help prevent manual handling injuries in the workplace, you should avoid such tasks as far as possible. Where it is not possible to avoid handling a load, employers must look at the risks of that task and put sensible health and safety measures in place to prevent and avoid injury, as shown in the following list and in Figure 1.5.

There are some simple things to do before and during the lift/carry.

STEP BY STEP — LIFTING AND CARRYING

- [ ] **Think before lifting/handling** – Plan the lift. Can handling aids be used? Where is the load going to be placed? Will help be needed with the load? Remove obstructions such as discarded wrapping materials. For a long lift, consider resting the load midway on a table or bench to change grip.
- [ ] **Adopt a stable position** – The feet should be apart with one leg slightly forward to maintain balance (alongside the load, if it is on the ground). Be prepared to move your feet during the lift to maintain your stability. Avoid tight clothing or unsuitable footwear, which may make this difficult.
- [ ] **Get a good hold** – Where possible, the load should be hugged as close as possible to the body. This may be better than gripping it tightly with hands only.
- [ ] **Start in a good posture** – At the start of the lift, slight bending of the back, hips and knees is preferable to fully flexing the back (stooping) or fully flexing the hips and knees (squatting).
- [ ] **Don't flex the back any further while lifting** – This can happen if the legs begin to straighten before starting to raise the load.
- [ ] **Keep the load close to the waist** – Keep the load close to the body for as long as possible while lifting. Keep the heaviest side of the load next to the body. If a close approach to the load is not possible, try to slide it towards the body before attempting to lift it.
- [ ] **Avoid twisting the back or leaning sideways, especially while the back is bent** – Shoulders should be kept level and facing in the same direction as the hips. Turning by moving the feet is better than twisting and lifting at the same time.
- [ ] **Keep the head up when handling** – Look ahead, not down at the load, once it has been held securely.
- [ ] **Move smoothly** – The load should not be jerked or snatched as this can make it harder to keep control and can increase the risk of injury.
- [ ] **Don't lift or handle more than you can easily manage** – There is a difference between what people can lift and what they can safely lift. If in doubt, seek advice or get help.
- [ ] **Put down, then adjust** – If precise positioning of the load is necessary, put it down first, then slide it into the desired position.

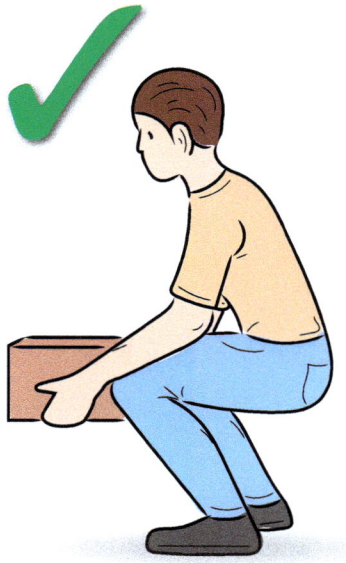
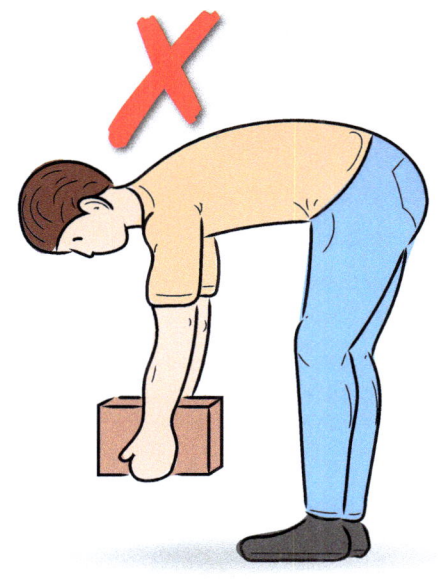

Figure 1.5: Always lift large parcels and loads in the correct manner; using an incorrect posture could lead to serious injury

Control of Substances Hazardous to Health Regulations (COSHH) 2002

COSHH covers substances that are hazardous to health. Your organisation should ensure that it assesses the risk of hazardous substances in use and takes appropriate action.

Hazardous substances can take many forms and include:
- chemicals and products containing chemicals
- fumes
- dusts
- mists
- gases
- biological agents (germs).

Once a chemical or hazardous substance has been identified, the employer must put identification labels on the container immediately if the correct labels are not already in place.

Use of work equipment

People and companies who own or operate work equipment are responsible for businesses and organisations whose employees use their work equipment.

Equipment provided for use at work should be:
- suitable for the intended use
- safe for use, maintained in a safe condition and inspected to ensure it is correctly installed and does not subsequently deteriorate
- used only by people who have received adequate information, instruction and training
- accompanied by suitable health and safety measures, such as protective devices and controls.

Assessment practice — A01 A03 A04

A business has a poor health and safety record. Senior managers have asked the health and safety department and its administrative team to produce a leaflet for all staff setting out their own and the employer's main responsibilities and identifying the procedures in place.

1. Explain two key health and safety responsibilities of an employee. (2 marks)
2. Identify one simple thing to do before or during lifting a box of photocopying paper. (1 mark)
3. Discuss the role of risk assessments in the maintenance of good health and safety in a working environment. (6 marks)

C3 Consumer rights

CONSUMERS are people who purchase goods and services for their own personal needs. They have rights to protect them from being sold faulty goods and services. As an administrator you may be asked to talk to a dissatisfied customer and you will need to be aware of their rights as a consumer.

Consumer Rights Act 2015

The Consumer Rights Act 2015 states that goods must be as described, fit for purpose and of satisfactory quality. For goods bought in a shop, during the expected lifespan of your product you are entitled to the following if the goods are faulty.

- Up to 30 days after the date of purchase – if your goods are faulty, you can get an immediate refund.
- Up to 6 months after the date of purchase – if a faulty product cannot be repaired or replaced, you are entitled to a full refund in most cases, though you may need to prove the fault was there when the product was first purchased.
- Up to 6 years after the date of purchase – if the goods do not last a reasonable length of time you may be entitled to some money back.

The next time you purchase an item, ask the sales assistant what the returns policy is

Your customer does not have a legal right to a refund or replacement because they simply change their mind. However, your organisation may have a policy on returned goods that does allow this.

> **Practise**
>
> If a customer made a complaint about a faulty good or service, what information about the purchase would you ask that customer to provide?

Consumer Contracts Regulations 2013

Where a customer has ordered goods from home, the Consumer Contracts Regulations 2013 say that (in most cases) the customer can cancel within 14 days. This is known as a 'cooling-off period'.

With regard to services, for example repair of a mobile phone, you can ask for a service to be repeated or fixed if it is not carried out with reasonable care and skills. Alternatively, you can get some money back if the problem caused by poor service cannot be fixed. If you haven't agreed a price for the service beforehand, what you are asked to pay must be reasonable. Similarly, if you haven't agreed a time, it must be carried out within a reasonable time period. As with goods bought online or ordered at home, you have a 14-day cooling-off period.

> **What if...?**
>
> Nigel Fargate bought a lawn mower from a well-known store 30 days ago. He was advised by a sales assistant that the mower he bought would be suitable for his garden. He has used the lawn mower several times and has come to the conclusion that it is not the right kind of lawn mower for him or his garden. He has brought the lawn mower back to the store and wants his money back.
>
> 1 Why is it important for the store and the staff to have a clear returns policy?
>
> 2 What could happen if the returns policy does not correspond with the Consumer Rights Act 2015?
>
> 3 If Nigel does not get a satisfactory response to his request what effect could it have on the business?

Digital content

The Consumer Rights Act 2015 also says digital content, for example a video game or app, must be as described, fit for purpose and of satisfactory quality. If the digital content is faulty, the customer is entitled to a repair or a replacement. If the fault can't be fixed, or if it hasn't been fixed within a reasonable time and without significant inconvenience, the customer can get some, or all, of their money back. Finally, if the fault has damaged the device itself the customer may be entitled to a repair or compensation. The Consumer Contracts Regulations 2013 say you have a right to change your mind within 14 days and get a full refund on your digital content. You do not have this right to cancel once a download has started, provided you have been told this and have acknowledged it.

C4 Equality and employment

All organisations have to be sure that their employees are treated fairly and equally. Organisations must ensure there is no **DISCRIMINATION** of any kind. Discrimination is defined as unfair treatment of a person, racial group or minority. This includes one employee making discriminatory remarks or gestures about another.

In your role as an administrator you need to have an understanding of discrimination regulations, both for your own benefit and to ensure you do not discriminate against others in the organisation. Such action could lead to you being disciplined.

Equality Act 2010

The aim of the Equality Act (EQA) is to improve equal job opportunities and fairness for employees and job applicants. Organisations should have policies in place to ensure this happens and to prevent discrimination.

Under the Act, it is unlawful to discriminate against people at work because of nine areas termed in the legislation as protected characteristics.

1. **Age** – the EQA makes it unlawful to discriminate against employees, job seekers and trainees because of age. For example, a business cannot favour one employee because they are 'younger' or 'older' than a relevant and comparable employee.
2. **Disability** – the EQA makes it unlawful to discriminate against employees because of a mental or physical disability.
3. **Gender reassignment** – gender reassignment is a personal, social and sometimes medical process by which a person's gender appears to others to have changed. Anyone who proposes to, starts or has completed a process to change their gender is protected from discrimination under the EQA. A person does not need to be undergoing medical supervision to be protected. For example, a woman who decides to live as a man, or vice versa, without undergoing any medical procedures would be covered.
4. **Marriage and civil partnership** – neither marriage nor civil partnership are defined in the Act, but the legislation is taken to broadly cover people who are married in a legally recognised union or in a legally recognised and registered civil partnership.
5. **Pregnancy and maternity** – it is unlawful to discriminate, or treat employees unfavourably, because of their pregnancy, or because they have given birth recently, are breastfeeding or on maternity leave. Discrimination happens when a woman is treated unfavourably because of pregnancy, pregnancy-related illness or because she exercises the right to statutory maternity leave.
6. **Race** – the EQA makes it unlawful to discriminate against employees, job seekers and trainees because of race. This includes the different elements of colour, nationality, and ethnic or national origin.
7. **Religion or belief** – it is unlawful to discriminate against anyone's belief or non-belief in any religion.
8. **Sex** – it is unlawful for an employer to discriminate against employees because of their sex. Sex discrimination against men is just as unlawful as sex discrimination against women.
9. **Sexual orientation** – it is unlawful to discriminate against employees, job seekers and trainees because of their sexual orientation. This includes gay, lesbian, bisexual or heterosexual individuals.

> **Practise**
>
> Design an appropriate poster advertising to other members of staff a training event on the Equality Act 2010. Your poster should explain why they need to attend the event.

Working Time Regulations 1998

The Working Time Regulations determine the maximum weekly working time, patterns of work and holidays, plus the permitted daily and weekly rest periods. The regulations apply to both part-time and full-time workers, including agency workers and **FREELANCERS** (self-employed people), although certain categories of workers are excluded.

In general the Working Time Regulations provide a right to:

- a limit of an average of 48 hours of work per week, though workers can choose to work longer by 'opting out'
- paid annual leave of 5.6 weeks a year including bank holidays
- 11 consecutive hours' rest in any 24-hour period
- a 20-minute rest break if the working day is longer than six hours
- one day off each week
- a limit on the normal working hours of night workers to an average eight hours in any 24-hour period, and an entitlement for night workers to receive regular health assessments.

There are special regulations for young workers, which restrict their working hours to 8 hours per day and 40 hours per week. The rest break is 30 minutes if their work lasts more than 4.5 hours. They are also entitled to two days off each week.

Employment Rights Act 1996

The primary aim of this Act is to provide basic employment protection for workers. The main areas and rules relate to:

Wages
- The Act establishes minimum procedures for making wage payments and makes unauthorised wage deductions illegal.
- It requires employers to make a 'guaranteed payment', even when the employer cannot find work for the employee.
- It establishes specific requirements for Sunday working.
- It requires the employer to provide a statement of employment (formally known as a contract of employment).

Time off work
- The Act entitles employees to paid holiday leave from commencement of employment.
- It entitles employees to have time off that may be owed as a result of personal needs such as antenatal care, training or public duties.
- It provides overarching guidance on the requirements for statutory maternity and paternity leave.

Dismissal and redundancy
- The Act lays down requirements that an organisation must adopt related to dismissal procedures.
- It provides the right to receive fair compensation in relation to cases of unfair dismissal from work.
- It provides the requirement for an employer to make payment in respect of redundancy.

Dispute resolution
- The Act lays down a requirement for a company to have a fair disciplinary and grievance procedure.
- It also provides the right for an employee to refer a dispute related to employment, dismissal, etc. to an employment tribunal.

Skills and knowledge check

☐ I can describe the main stages of a risk assessment.
☐ I can identify what groups are protected by the Equality Act 2010.
☐ I can correctly and safely lift and carry boxes and heavy parcels.
☐ I understand the rights of consumers based on my knowledge of the Consumer Rights Act 2015.

○ I can list the eight rules or principles of data protection.
○ I know what is meant by COSHH.
○ I know what my main health and safety responsibilities at work are.
○ I know what the specific aspects of the Working Time Regulations are that refer to the working week.

D The structure in which the organisation operates

D1 Ownership

The role of an administrator is an important one and is found in all types of organisations across the private, public and not for profit sectors. Your role may differ depending on what type of organisation you work for.

The private sector

In this sector organisations are businesses that are owned by individuals. The business is organised in such a way as to make a profit for its owners. Within this sector are the following business types.

Sole trader

A **SOLE TRADER** is the most common type of business. It is owned and controlled by one person, and the role of the administrator is to support and respond to the instructions of the owner. An administrator here would find themselves doing a wide variety of tasks.

Partnership

A **PARTNERSHIP** is a type of business where two or more people own and control the business. They work together and have to agree how profit or losses are shared. Here you could be reporting to one or all of the partners. You may find you have a wide variety of tasks to complete if the partnership is a small one with a small administration team.

Public and private limited companies

Limited companies are incorporated. This means the owners or shareholders are only liable for losses up to the value of the shares they hold in the business. In addition, the company has its own legal identity and it can sue or be sued, buy property, make contracts and so on in its own name. Private limited companies have one or more shareholders and the shares they hold in the business are 'private' to them. In contrast public limited companies have at least two shareholders and are required to 'issue' at least £50,000 of shares to members of the public at large. The value of these shares will be published on the London Stock Exchange for all to see and shares can be traded, i.e. bought and sold on the stock exchange.

Cooperatives

This type of business is owned by its employees and potentially its customers and suppliers as well. The business aims and objectives will be influenced by ethical and moral concerns, for example the environment or fair trade.

The public sector

The public sector is made up of organisations and departments run by central or local government. Their role is to provide vital services for the public, such as education and cleaning services. They are financed through the raising of taxes, for example income tax. They are not required to make a profit but have to be efficient and offer good value for money.

Public corporations

A public corporation is set up by the government to deliver a public service, for example Network Rail. A corporation will have a board of directors who determine what has to be done to achieve the aims and objectives set out for it by the government.

Not for profit organisations

These organisations provide and sell products and services but are not run to make a profit. All income is spent on running the organisation and providing for the reason for the existence of that organisation. Charities, for instance, get donations or sell goods to provide the funds to support their chosen area.

This sector also includes businesses and organisations in the voluntary sector such as volunteer community associations, hospital volunteer groups and Neighbourhood Watch.

Your role as an administrator will be influenced by the type of organisation you are working for. However the core activities of your role, as identified earlier in this section, will be similar no matter where you are employed.

D2 Size

As an administrator you will have to be familiar with a number of technical terms used by colleagues. The sizes of organisations are described by the terms shown in Table 1.7.

Table 1.7: Organisation sizes

Organisation	Size of organisation
Micro business	A micro business has between 1 and 9 employees.
Small and Medium Size Enterprises (SME)	A small business has between 10 and 49 employees. A medium business has between 50 and 249 employees.
Large organisation	A large organisation has 250 or more employees.

The size and/or type of business will influence and be influenced by the scope of its business activities.

The use of the internet has allowed even small businesses access to a bigger market than they may have had previously. The delivery services you learnt about earlier would be used to deliver goods to their customers.

D3 Structure

A third major aspect of how organisations are set up and run is how they are structured. All organisations need some form of structure. Structure refers to how tasks and responsibilities are allocated to different job roles, and how these roles are put into different teams and departments. In addition there are different levels of supervision and management with varying degrees of authority; this is known as **HIERARCHY**. Once the structure is in place, all activities have to be managed together in a co-ordinated and orderly way.

Flat structures

Organisations with **FLAT STRUCTURES**, as shown in Figure 1.6, have only two or three levels of hierarchy. As a result, there is much interaction between staff and sharing of information and ideas across levels. There tends to be less direct supervision by managers, so you will find as an administrator you have more freedom to act and take your own decisions. Generally these kind of businesses react quickly to the needs of their customers and staff. You will find flat structures in micro and small businesses.

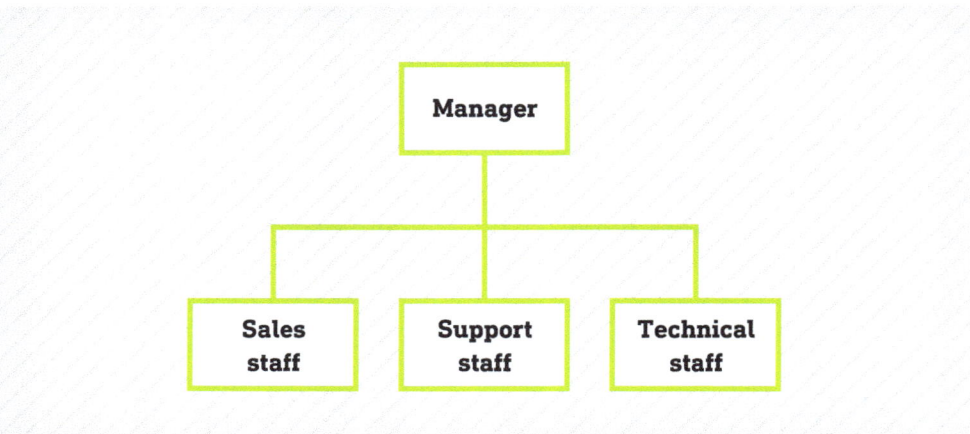

Figure 1.6: A flat structure

Tall structures

TALL STRUCTURES have many levels of hierarchy with many managers and supervisors, each with their own area of responsibility and teams. The teams they supervise and manage, and the individuals within them, will have specific tasks and clearly defined and focused responsibilities. They are required to closely follow the rules and procedures laid down by the organisation and its managers. Medium and large organisations use this kind of structure, for example, local and central government organisations and international and national banks.

An example of a tall structure in an organisation is shown in Figure 1.7.

Figure 1.7: A tall structure

Hierarchical structures

HIERARCHICAL STRUCTURES tend to have many layers of management at the top of the organisation, but towards the bottom of the organisation the **SPAN OF CONTROL** (the number of staff one person directly supervises) increases. It could be said therefore that this is a mix of a tall and flat structure.

Look at Figure 1.8 for an example of a hierarchical structure. Then look back at Figures 1.6 and 1.7 and see if you can identify similarities with the hierarchical structure.

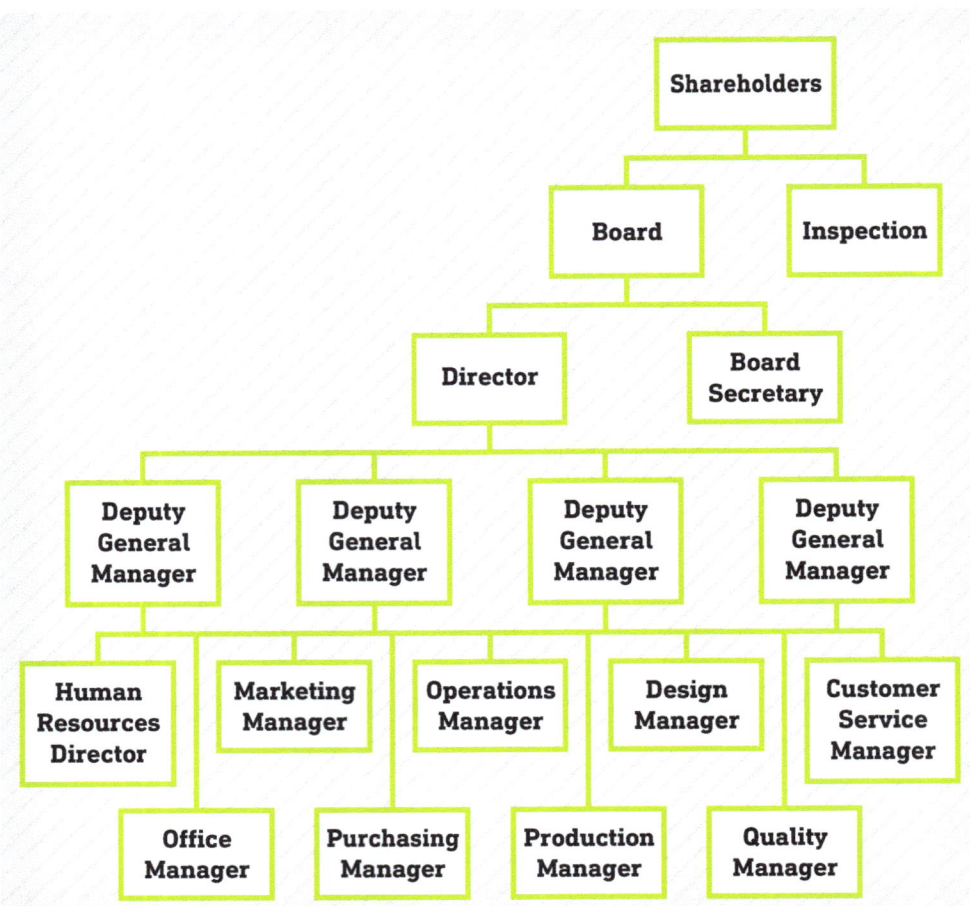

Figure 1.8: A hierarchical structure brings together elements of both flat and tall structures

Matrix structures

A **MATRIX STRUCTURE**, as shown in Figure 1.9, is often used when the organisation is involved in a number of big projects. Each project has a team of people brought together from across the organisation with the necessary skills and experience to complete the project successfully.

The other specialist functions, such as marketing, finance or human resources, are used to support each team as and when required. The team will have its own head or leader. Once the project is completed the team is disbanded and the staff will go back to their original functions or join another team.

This type of structure is found in medium or large organisations that operate on a national or international level, for example, civil engineers who build bridges, roads and large buildings and skyscrapers. You could be tasked with supporting one of these teams on a temporary basis.

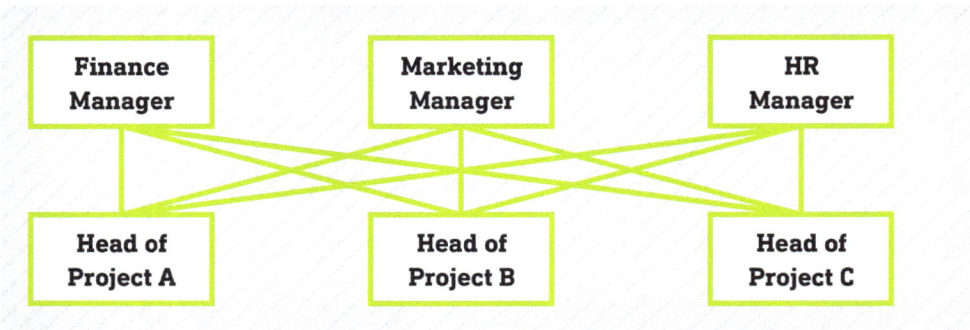

Figure 1.9: A matrix structure

Functional structures

The organisation is divided into specialist or functional areas, for example human resources (HR), administration, sales or finance. **FUNCTIONAL STRUCTURES**, as shown in Figure 1.10, allow teams and individuals to become specialists and experts in one particular aspect of the business and its activities.

It is clear to all employees and customers who they need to communicate with to get information and advice about particular areas of the business. It is still important that these functions have clear links to each other and that they work together to achieve the aims and objectives of the organisation.

This type of structure is found in SMEs and large organisations. Your role here would be specialised within one of these functions.

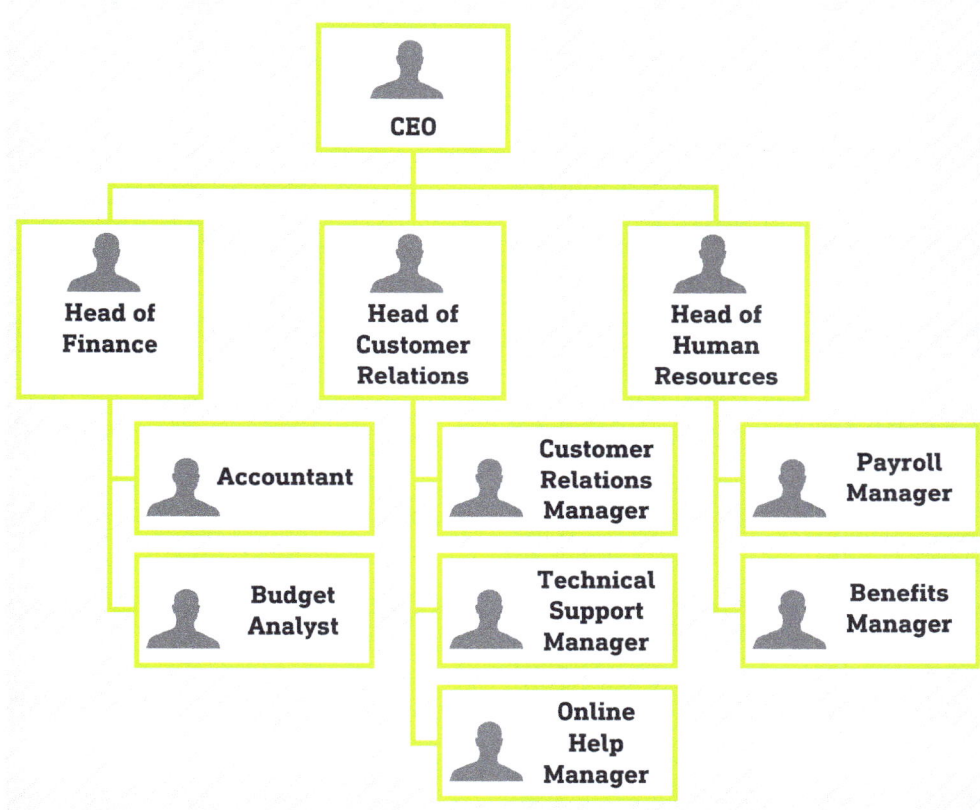

Figure 1.10: What are the advantages to staff of a functonal structure?

Assessment practice — A01 A04

Two friends have set up a business together to manufacture and sell handmade wooden toys in their home town.

1. Identify the type of ownership of this business. (1 mark)
2. Explain the size and structure of the business. (2 marks)
3. Discuss how this business would affect the role and responsibilities of an employed administrator. (6 marks)

Skills and knowledge check

☐ I can describe the three different sectors in the UK economy.
☐ I can explain the main differences between a sole trader and a partnership.
☐ I can describe what a public limited company has to do that a private limited company does not.

○ I know what an SME is and how many employees it has.
○ I know what kind of structure has many levels.
○ I understand the advantages of different types of organisation structures.
○ I understand how the size of an organisation affects its structure.
○ I know how my role as an administrator might change in different types of businesses.

WORK FOCUS

HANDS ON

There are some important technical and professional skills and competencies that you will need to practise which relate to this unit and your role as an administrator. Developing and practising these will help you make a good impression in your work experience as well as gaining employment in the future.

Using different types of office equipment

- For all the types of office equipment you use in your work experience, try to find the manuals and index them accordingly. Ensure that your colleagues know where they can be located and that they are accessible.

- Select two business-type photocopiers, either online or ones that you use or have used personally. Identify the brand name and key features and compare the two using an appropriate format, for example a table. Present this to your supervisor.

Use appropriate communication methods in a business or working environment

- Keep a log of any contact you have with customers or your tutor for one week and analyse the methods of communication you used. Say why each method was effective or, on reflection, whether another method should have been used.

Work effectively as part of a team

- For a work or social team, list all the members and identify the particular skills they bring to the team.

- Look for opportunities to support another team member in achieving a goal or target. Record your actions.

Understanding organisation structure

- Draw the organisational structure of your college, school or work placement, identifying the main levels and roles.

Ready for work?

Imagine you work for a small graphic design and printing business with 30 employees. The business wants to promote itself within the town in which it is located. You have been asked to be part of a project team who want to link up with local community groups to adopt two areas of waste ground and convert them into play and recreation areas.

- Identify two skills that you would bring to the team and how they would be used to benefit the team.
- What methods of communication would be best used to make contact with local community groups initially?
- In face-to-face meetings with the community group or its representatives, what non-verbal communication skills and techniques can you use to ensure a good relationship is developed?
- How would you ensure there is no misunderstanding between your business and the community groups?
- Once the work has begun, what health and safety regulations would apply?
- What office equipment should be made available by your business to ensure the project is successful?

Getting ready for assessment

This section has been written to help you do your best when you sit the assessment test for this unit. Read through it carefully and ask your tutor if there is anything you are still not sure about.

About the test

What to expect in the test

At the end of the unit you will be assessed using an onscreen test.

- Read the questions carefully. You may need to read the question more than once to fully understand it.
- Plan your time during the exam. Allocating a set amount of time per question is one way of doing this. For example if there are 20 questions then around four minutes per question is a rough guide. Alternatively, you could aim to spend around one minute per mark – so you could allow six minutes for a question that has been allocated six marks.
- If you are stuck on a particular question, you should move on to the next one – don't waste time through confusion and uncertainty. If you have time, you can go back to the question later. You should make a note of any questions you have not answered so you do not forget.
- Before you submit your answers, quickly check that you are happy with them.
- Remember, you will not lose marks for an incorrect answer so it is better to guess the answer rather than leaving it blank.

Your tutor will provide you with information about the number of marks available, as well as how much time you will be given to complete the test. You can also find this information and sample assessments on the Pearson Qualifications website (qualifications.pearson.com/qualifications), by searching for Business Administration under BTEC Level 2 Technicals.

Understanding the questions

The test contains different types of questions. There will be both multiple choice and short answer questions based on a concise, realistic scenario similar to one you might come across as an administrator. The multiple choice questions will require you to pick one answer from four options or sometimes two from five.

Where you are expected to provide short answers, you will see particular 'command' words that you must follow. The following table lists these words and describes how you should answer questions that include them. Please note that not every word will be used in every test.

Command	Definition
Analyse	You need to examine the meaning or essential features of a topic or situation in detail, or break something down into its components to say how they are related and consider their importance.
Assess	You need to carefully consider all factors or events that apply to a specific situation.
Complete	You are required to add information, for example, to complete a table, graph, chart or missing word or phrase from a sentence/statement.
Discuss	You need to consider all the different aspects of a topic, how they interrelate and the extent to which they are important.
Evaluate	You need to review all the information provided to consider aspects such as strengths or weaknesses, advantages or disadvantages, alternative actions, and relevance or significance, and come to a conclusion.

UNIT 1 | UNDERSTANDING ADMINISTRATIVE SERVICES

Command	Definition
Explain	You are required to give reasons to support an opinion, view or argument, with clear details.
Identify, name, outline, state, give	These terms require you to give a brief, precise response, term or definition without going into a lot of detail.
Match	You must choose a thing that resembles or corresponds to another, to make a similar or complementary pair.

Sample questions and answers

Knowledge and understanding

These types of questions assess your knowledge and understanding of the unit content. Q1 assesses your understanding of section A in Unit 1 and Q2 section B. For these types of questions, you must ensure you have revised the unit content. You should also be clear about what the command words are asking you to do and make sure you apply this to your answer.

Question 1

Which legislation protects employees who have embarked on gender reassignment from discriminatory employment practices? (1 mark)

Select **one** option.

☐ Consumer Rights Act 2015
☐ Health and Safety at Work Act 1974
☐ Equality Act 2010
☐ Data Protection Act 1998

Question 2

A large company has a number of big projects that need to be completed.

Which of the following structures is the best option for this? (1 mark)

Select **one** option.

☐ Functional
☐ Tall
☐ Public sector
☐ Matrix

Question 3

James Hammond is a senior administrator for an international company. Some of the senior managers will be travelling to their office in Paris, France for a meeting in seven days' time. He has to make all the travel arrangements for the trip. In addition, he has to send 5 kg of publicity samples to Paris in advance of the meeting.

Explain one factor that will affect the choice of delivery service. (4 marks)

Sample answer

The urgency of the delivery is an important factor.

Verdict

This is not a good answer because the factor has been identified but not explained.

Sample answer

Proof of delivery is a factor so in this case the sender will have to use recorded delivery.

Verdict

This is a good answer because:

- the factor has been identified
- there is an explanation of how this affects the choice of service.

Question 4

Refer back to the scenario in Question 3. Discuss the problems that can arise when planning business travel and their potential impact on the business. (6 marks)

Sample answer

Unclear communication could have a negative impact on the business. For example the travellers may arrive at the station or airport too late and miss the train or plane. The reputation of the business will decline if they miss their appointments with clients.

Verdict

This is not a very good answer because:

- only one key aspect has been identified in detail
- the points made are generic and not directly linked to the situation given in the question.

Sample answer

Unclear communications will have a negative effect on the meeting, and most importantly, a major impact on the business. For example, if it is not made clear that the parcel has to be in France in time for the meeting, there will be no publicity materials to leave for prospective clients, and business and profits may be lost.

Delays and cancellations could negatively affect the business. If a train or plane is delayed by bad weather in the UK but not in France then the clients will have to be informed of the problems and alternative arrangements made urgently to save the reputation of the company. This may be the most difficult problem to predict and plan for.

A lack of resources could cause problems because if there are a number of people travelling, a limited budget may mean the choice of travel is limited; for example, planes or trains would be more expensive than travelling together in a car on a ferry. However, driving will take longer and there may be accidents and hold ups along the route.

Another problem might arise if any of the travellers have an expired passport. It could negatively impact the meeting for everyone if a key participant cannot travel. However, this problem is more easily avoided if travellers are asked to check their passports well in advance.

Verdict

This is an excellent answer because:
- a range of problems is identified
- some key aspects are explained in depth
- the majority of points made are relevant
- there is a clear link to the scenario
- the importance and impact of most problems is weighed up.

Question 5

Holly Williams is an administrator at a large national business. She has been asked to inform all managers of an important forthcoming meeting in London that all will be required to attend.

Explain two different methods of communication Holly might use within her business to inform the required attendees about the forthcoming meeting.
(4 marks)

Sample answer

Emails and memos could be used to tell managers about the meeting.

Verdict

This is not a good answer because, although two possible methods have been given, there is no explanation for why the methods would be used.

Sample answer

Email would be a good method to tell managers of this meeting as it will be easy to circulate the message to everyone and an email is a permanent reminder of the meeting. A memo could also be used as this would be short but would include all details of the meeting. Managers would have a permanent copy for their records. The memos could be sent by email or a hard copy could be sent by internal mail.

Verdict

This is a good answer because:
- it states two correct methods
- it clearly explains why these are good methods.

Question 6

Refer back to the scenario in Question 5. Explain the negative impact on the business if, as a result of poor communication and mistakes, Holly missed some managers off the mailing list. (4 marks)

Sample answer

A negative impact might be complaints about some managers from their colleagues.

Verdict

This is not a good answer as it does not explain what the result would be if managers did not receive the information.

Sample answer

This information ensures that all managers will make themselves available for the meeting. If some do not get the information in good time, they may not be able to make arrangements to get to the meeting and their colleagues may think they have deliberately not attended the meeting. In addition, there may be important clients at the meeting who will also be disappointed if managers do not turn up to meet them.

Verdict

This is a good answer because:

- it identifies the impact the mistakes may have on the operations of the business
- it clearly indicates why that may be the case
- it highlights the overall costs to the business.

Answers to Assessment practice questions

Shown below are suggested answers to questions in Assessment practice features in Unit 1.

Unit 1

Assessment practice, page 13

(1 mark for each correct match)

scanner – to convert hard copy documents in to computer files. (1 mark)

shredder – to destroy confidential documents no longer needed. (1 mark)

Assessment practice, page 27

Acceptable answer:

(1 mark for stating the skill and 1 mark for saying why this is important in becoming a good team member)

To be able to meet agreed deadlines (1) because you will be expected to be motivated and do all you can to meet your targets. (1)

OR

To be able to co-operate with other team members (1) and be able to contribute and, if necessary, work with them to meet the targets for the whole team over and above your own. (1)

Assessment practice, page 34

1. Acceptable answer:
   - To take care of your own health and safety and that of others by working in a safe and sensible way at all times. (1)
   - Not to use safety equipment incorrectly or maliciously, for example fire extinguishers or fire blankets. (1)
2. Acceptable answer:
   - Adopt a stable position. (1)

   OR
   - Hold the box close to your waist. (1)

   OR
   - Do not lift more than you can comfortably carry either by size or weight. (1)
3. *(Answers may cover all or some of the indicative content, but should be rewarded for other relevant answers. An acceptable answer might include some of the following, up to a maximum of 6 marks)*
   - A brief definition of risk assessment. (1)
   - An outline of the legal responsibility of a business with regard to risk assessments. (1)
   - An outline of the role of employees in the risk assessment process. (1)
   - An explanation of the stages of a risk assessment. (2)
   - The impact on the business as a whole of a good risk assessment process. (2)
   - The impact on the business as a whole of a poor risk assessment process. (2)

Assessment practice, page 44

1. Acceptable answer: A Partnership. (1)
2. Acceptable answer:

   (1 mark for correctly identifying each of the measures, up to a maximum of 2 marks.)
   - The size of the business is that of a micro business (1) with less than 10 members of staff. (1)
   - The structure of the business is a flat structure (1) which means there are few levels of hierarchy. (1)
3. *(Answers may cover all or some of the indicative content, but should be rewarded for other relevant answers. An acceptable answer might include some of the following, up to a maximum of 6 marks)*
   - The variety of tasks will be different. (1)

   OR
   - Because of the type of structure, the administrator will have a wider variety of tasks to complete because there will not be other specialist functions or departments to take on these tasks. (2)
   - The interaction between staff will be different. (1)

   OR
   - Because of the size of the business and the small number of staff, the interaction between individual staff will be increased as they need to work more closely together. (2)
   - The freedom to act and make your own decisions will be affected. (1)

   OR
   - Because there will be less direct supervision as the partners will be busy, the administrator will have to act more on their own initiative and make decisions for themselves. (2)
   - A comparison of the roles and responsibilities of an administrator in this structure with that of another structure. (2)

2 Providing Administrative Services

Have you ever wondered what would happen if an organisation didn't have administrators to carry out agreed tasks on a daily basis? How long do you think an organisation would survive without administrative support to enable it to meet targets?

This unit explores a range of administrative duties; these include managing information, handling mail, supporting meetings, and meeting and greeting visitors. You will be shown how to work safely and effectively within an office environment and work with others in a responsible and professional manner. You will develop transferable skills and knowledge to help you prepare for future employment as an administrator, and learn how this important role contributes to the success of an organisation.

How will I be assessed?

You will be assessed through the submission of observation records, completed and signed by an assessor, and 'witness statements', produced by experienced administrative staff who have observed you carrying out administrative duties. Observation records and witness statements must be accompanied by relevant supporting evidence for assessment.

The documentation that you produce while you are working through this unit will provide you with further supporting evidence that you can use for your assessments. In addition, you will be given the opportunity to create a presentation or produce information leaflets that will demonstrate your knowledge and understanding of the roles and responsibilities of an administrator.

The table below shows you the criteria that will be used to assess you.

Assessment criteria

Pass	Merit	Distinction
Learning aim A: Carry out routine administrative activities to meet requirements		
A.P1 Follow instructions to carry out at least three routine administrative activities to meet requirements.	**A.M1** Carry out at least three routine administrative activities in line with requirements, demonstrating experience and procedural knowledge in their approach.	**A.D1** Carry out at least three routine administrative activities competently in line with requirements, demonstrating confidence and consistency in their approach.
A.P2 Outline how to manage time and task to ensure requirements are met on completion.	**A.M2** Describe different time management tools and task-taking techniques that are used to ensure tasks are completed in line with requirements.	**A.D2** Explain how to effectively manage time and tasks through the use of tools and techniques, including actions that can be taken to minimise interruptions and distractions.
Learning aim B: Use office equipment safely and in line with procedures		
B.P3 Use at least three different types of office equipment safely, following instructions and procedures.	**B.M3** Select and use at least three different types of office equipment safely, in line with instructions and procedures.	**B.D3** Select and use at least three different types of office equipment safely and competently, in line with organisational instructions and procedures, demonstrating the ability to resolve occurring problems.
Learning aim C: Demonstrate professional behaviours and effective communication in the work environment		
C.P4 Communicate effectively with others using acceptable and appropriate written, verbal and non-verbal communication skills and techniques.	**C.M4** Act in an exemplary manner in the work environment and demonstrate good written, verbal and non-verbal communication skills that are appropriate to the situations.	**C.D4** Act in an exemplary manner in the work environment and consistently demonstrate professional written, verbal and non-verbal communication skills that are appropriate to the situations.
C.P5 Demonstrate acceptable and appropriate behaviours in the work environment.		

A Carry out routine administrative activities to meet requirements

A1 Types of administrative activities

This section explores the roles and responsibilities of an administrator. While there are many similarities across organisations, some activities may vary depending upon the size, nature and requirements of each individual business.

The role of an administrator is to carry out activities that support colleagues throughout the department or organisation. An administrator assists in the day-to-day running of a workspace within an organisation. Some typical administrative activities are:

- dealing with incoming and outgoing COMMUNICATIONS
- managing diaries and appointments
- organising business meetings
- reception duties
- arranging business trips
- storing and retrieving information.

A PROCEDURE is a set of step-by-step instructions that should be followed by everyone so that a task is completed successfully and in the format required by the business. Organisations often present procedures in the form of a document so they can be easily referred to and shared with others. Procedures should exist for each of the activities listed above.

Having procedures in place will allow everyone to work towards the same standard of quality in exactly the same way. This will enable you to meet the requirements of the organisation. When you follow a procedure, you will be adopting a step-by-step approach to fulfilling an administrative task.

What routine activities would you carry out as an administrator?

Handling mail

You may be surprised at the large number of letters and packages that will need to be opened and sorted through on a daily basis in an organisation. Naturally, the larger the organisation, the more mail there will be to open and sort through. Some very large organisations may have a dedicated 'post room' or 'mail room', but in smaller businesses mail duties are likely to be carried out by the receptionist.

Incoming mail

An administrator tasked with sorting through letters and packages that have been received will carry out the following activities.

- Unless addressed to a named colleague, each envelope will be opened and the contents will be removed. The letters/contents removed from the envelope will be stamped as 'received' so that all letters show a date of receipt.
- If an envelope is addressed to a particular named colleague, it will be left unopened and handed to that person later (or placed in their PIGEONHOLE). The same applies to envelopes marked as 'Confidential'.
- If a letter or CIRCULAR (a document that is circulated within the organisation) needs to be read by several members of staff, it will be attached to a circulation slip and sent to the appropriate colleagues for each of them to read. Each colleague will sign the circulation slip once they have read the attachment. They will then pass the slip and the attachment to the next colleague who is listed on the circulation slip.
- Once they have been sorted, all letters received in the mail room (or at reception) will be distributed to appropriate staff members or placed in their individual pigeonholes for them to collect.
- Payments made by cheque that come into the organisation must be logged according to the organisation's procedures. The cheque must then be stapled to the original letter and handed to the correct person within the organisation, for example the finance department.
- There should be specific procedures in place to deal with suspicious parcels or letters that arrive at the organisation. It is likely that training will be given to you so you know exactly what to do and it is very important that procedures are followed carefully. This will help to ensure that everyone is kept safe.

It is very important that the mail you have sorted reaches staff members as quickly as possible. This is so that colleagues can respond promptly to the sender of the letter or carry out any other instructions.

Outgoing mail

You will need to collect your colleagues' outgoing letters and packages from the 'outboxes' located in each department's office. Once back at the mail room or reception, the letters and packages you have collected will need to be arranged by priority into first-class or second-class categories, ready for dispatch.

It is important that outgoing mail is collected from all of the organisation's outboxes mid-afternoon or in line with your organisation's procedures. This will give you enough time to prepare the mail ready for the collection deadlines offered by Royal Mail or the courier collection service.

Sorting and preparing outgoing mail

Your organisation may train you to use a franking machine when you are dealing with outgoing mail. The machine will print a symbol onto letters so you do not need to attach a postage stamp.

Large letters and packages need to be weighed and measured. This will establish how much it will cost to post the items and will dictate which 'label' should be used, as shown in Figure 2.1. This in turn will ensure that all letters and parcels are correctly prepared ready for collection.

Organisations will have their own preferred mail and parcel delivery services that they use and will display their current prices on a wall chart or a print-off from the internet.

If you are sending parcels or letters overseas you will need to make sure the item is packaged securely. Place an address label on the parcel that clearly shows the name and address of the recipient, use an 'Airmail' label, apply an international 'track and sign' barcode if tracking is necessary and complete a 'Customs declaration' label, describing the contents.

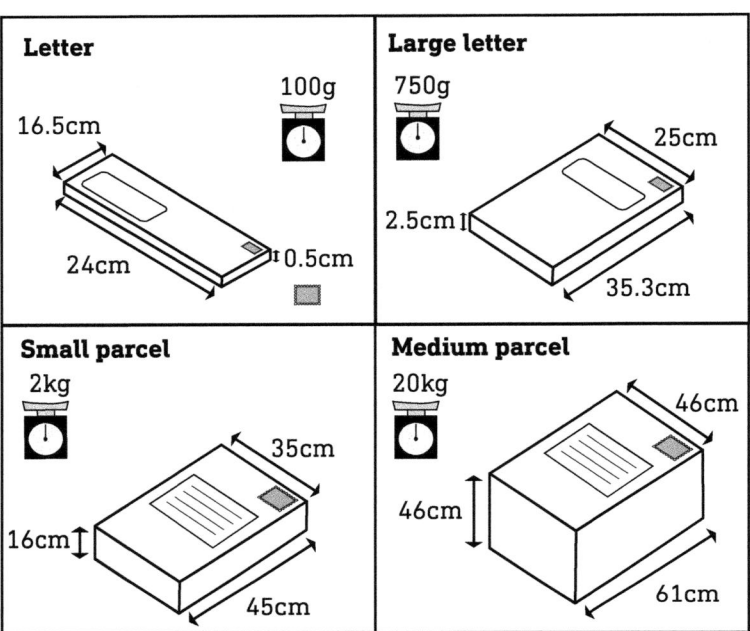

Figure 2.1: Royal Mail parcel and letter size guide

Late outgoing mail

Outgoing mail must be ready to leave the organisation on time each day. Mail that is not ready will be held in the mail room until the next day. This can result in disappointed or upset customers, which is not good for the reputation of the organisation. You have probably experienced waiting for a parcel to arrive at your house and, if so, you will know how frustrating it can be if it is late.

Whoever is in charge of handling mail should do everything they can to ensure mail reaches recipients on time. One way to do this is to ensure letters and packages are addressed and labelled correctly and accurately.

Sending a parcel

Table 2.1 lists some examples of resources and information you might need if you are required to send a fragile component to a customer using the Royal Mail Special Delivery Guaranteed service.

Tools and equipment	Information needed
Packing tape	Name of customer
Packing box	Address of destination
Packing paper/bag	Whether confirmation of delivery is required
Clear document wallet	Speed of delivery
Bubble wrap	
Scales	
Fragile labels	
Tape measure	

Table 2.1: Checklist for sending a parcel

Practise

1. Spend some time looking at the Royal Mail website to find out how to package a parcel safely and correctly ready for posting.
2. Produce a leaflet for colleagues to use, highlighting the steps they must take to prepare a parcel for posting.

Practise

1. Make a list of different courier and postal services that might be used by businesses.
2. What UK postal services do different postal companies and couriers offer?
3. What international postal services do different postal companies and couriers offer?

Diaries and appointments

Diaries are very useful tools to help with the planning and management of everyone's time within an organisation. In most offices you will find that some employees prefer to use manual diaries, some prefer to use electronic diaries and others use both. Each type has advantages and disadvantages, as shown in Table 2.2.

Diary type	Advantages	Disadvantages
Manual	• Quick and easy to write in • Amendments can be made quickly • Doesn't require batteries or charging points	• Only one person can use it at a time • Can get lost • Other people can see the information
Electronic	• Can be shared with other staff easily • You can synchronise data across different electronic systems • You can organise appointments in collaboration • You can set meeting reminders	• Needs batteries or power • If computer or mobile phone 'crashes' you may lose data • Can be hacked into • May need Wi-Fi or mobile data to synchronise

Table 2.2: Advantages and disacvantages of electronic and manual diaries

> **Practise**
>
> Look at a manual diary and an electronic diary (for example, Outlook) and write down a list of the information you can input easily.

It is very important to manage time effectively in a business setting. Time is a very important resource and must be managed properly to enable staff to meet their targets. This helps everyone to be more productive, which improves performance throughout the organisation.

Managing diary entries and appointments

Figure 2.2 shows some of the different types of diary entries. Generally, administrators are expected to manage diaries in the following ways.

- All meetings and appointments must be recorded accurately in a manual or electronic diary. You will need to record the name and contact details, including a telephone number, of the person who is requesting the appointment.
- Ensure the time and date of the meeting do not clash with any other appointments by checking the schedules of all those invited. Make sure colleagues have enough time to travel between appointments.
- Prioritise appointments so that the most urgent meetings are arranged before less important ones. Remember to inform other colleagues if a less important meeting is postponed until another time. Send out meeting invitations in good time.
- Make sure everybody who needs to be at the meeting knows about it in good time and is aware of what they might need to bring.

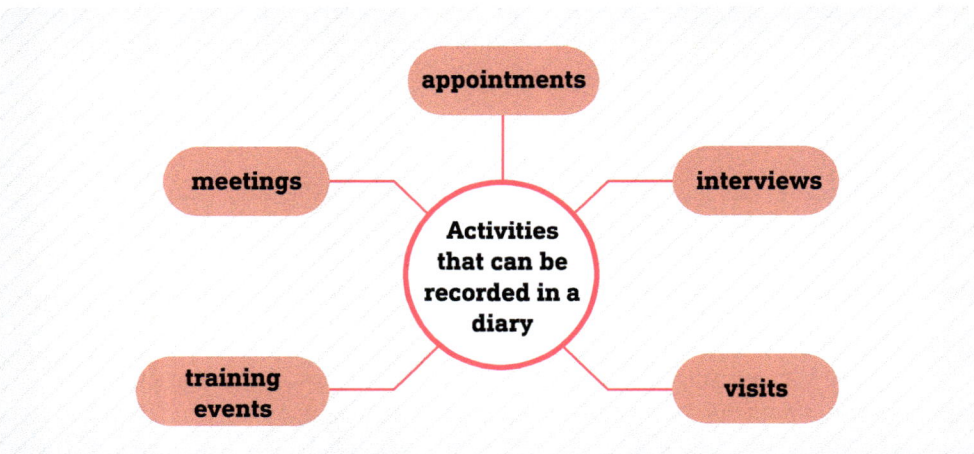

Figure 2.2: What other activities might you enter into your workplace diary?

Managing appointments at reception

A large diary is likely to be kept at reception so that the receptionist or administrator knows where staff members will be at any particular time and when to expect visitors who have made appointments. Alternatively, the receptionist may use an electronic diary on a computer. Different organisations will have either one or both systems in use. Having this information is useful if an internal or external customer contacts reception, asking to speak to a colleague.

The administrator will usually have been informed if a colleague has arranged a visit from an external client for a business appointment. Details of who is expected, and when, will be recorded in the diary. Once the visitor arrives, the administrator will notify the appropriate staff member and will then make the visitor feel welcome while they wait.

There will be occasions, however, when visitors arrive without an appointment. This can be problematic because the person they ask to see may be busy or in an important meeting. This can happen when, for example, a sales representative calls at the organisation without an appointment.

Gatekeeping

The term **GATEKEEPING** refers to an administrator preventing a visitor from seeing a colleague without an appointment if the visit is not of an urgent nature. The administrator will check the diary and offer to make an appointment for the visitor to see the colleague at a convenient time.

How can a diary be used to prioritise activities?

A receptionist or a **PA** (personal assistant – an administrator who works exclusively for one particular person) will need to know where key colleagues will be located throughout the working day. This is so they can contact them if there are any telephone calls that need an urgent response.

Communicating diary entries

At reception, messages will often be taken over the telephone. If the receptionist has access to colleagues' diaries they may enter appointments in suitable free slots. Colleagues will see these appointments next time they look at their diary.

Cancellations or changes to appointments must be communicated to staff members when necessary. A receptionist may pass on telephone messages by email, or they may write them down and put them in the relevant colleague's pigeonhole. The colleague can then contact the caller directly to arrange an appointment and enter this appointment in their diary.

Remember different organisations have different workplace cultures (the way things are done within an organisation). This means that procedures and processes may differ.

Keeping up-to-date and **ACCURATE** diaries and arranging appointments properly will help colleagues to monitor their workloads. This helps to keep everyone up to date and aware of any changes.

Supporting meetings

If you are invited to a meeting in the workplace, you will need to know the venue, time and date, as well as information about the purpose of the meeting.

Informal meetings

You may have already attended an informal meeting, perhaps in school, college, a voluntary organisation or the workplace. Examples of informal meetings in the workplace include team briefings or debriefings, monthly supervision meetings or committee meetings.

Formal meetings

Formal meetings are held in a less relaxed atmosphere where very important decisions will be made that could affect the whole organisation, and its employees. An example of a formal meeting is a senior management team meeting or perhaps a **BOARD OF DIRECTORS** meeting. A Board of Directors is a team of senior members of staff in a company who make plans and decisions to drive the organisation forward.

When arranging a formal meeting the following documents will be needed:

- terms of reference
- invitations to attend
- an attendance list
- copies of **MINUTES** of the previous meeting
- a **CHAIRPERSON'S AGENDA**
- agendas
- copies of reports or other documents to be distributed during the meeting.

Organising meetings

When you are asked to organise a meeting you will need to carry out the following tasks.

- Create invitations and send these out to attendees and ask them to confirm their attendance by a certain date and to inform you of any special needs or requirements they may have.
- Once you have received confirmation from those who are attending, send out agendas, previous minutes and directions to the venue.
- Book a suitable room that will be large enough to comfortably accommodate everyone who is attending, using the organisation's booking procedures. Consider the layout of the meeting room. Make sure you have considered any special needs such as wheelchair access.
- Book equipment that may be required such as laptops or projectors. Check the room before the meeting to ensure there are no trailing wires or any other health and safety concerns.
- Book refreshments so they are available as delegates arrive and are sufficient for the duration of the meeting. Consider any special dietary requirements.
- Make sure that necessary paperwork and accessories such as delegate packs, attendance lists and name badges have been prepared accordingly.
- Make sure there is sufficient car parking for external guests.

After the meeting, make sure the room has been left tidy, clean and safe ready for the next users. Make sure any equipment that was used has been returned. If you were allocated the role of minute-taker, you will need to type up the minutes and distribute them to all attendees and those who were unable to attend. Follow up the actions that were allocated to attendees during the meeting and, in some cases, liaise with the chairperson to make sure the actions are carried out.

Often a 'checklist' will be used to make sure that all these points have been considered. The checklist can be ticked and initialled as each item on the list is actioned. This is a good way to plan a meeting and to make sure that nothing is forgotten.

Arranging meetings away from your workplace

When arranging an external meeting it is important to visit the meeting room beforehand to establish its suitability. All attendees will want to feel comfortable, especially if a long meeting is planned.

You will need to ensure that:
- water jugs and glasses are available
- there is adequate ventilation
- there is room for adequate refreshments to be placed in the room
- lighting is sufficient
- dietary needs have been considered
- there is signposting for toilets and designated smoking areas.

Written confirmation of the bookings and authorisation from a manager may be necessary. This is very important when **BUDGETS** are in place.

Likewise, it is always a good idea to ask whether the chairperson or anyone else involved with the meeting (especially external guests) will require additional resources such as flip chart stands and paper, pens or perhaps laptops.

Timely and accurate communication is essential to make sure all attendees, including the chairperson and minute-taker, can place the meeting in their diaries so that they can plan ahead.

Link it up

Go to Unit 1, Section A1, to see an example of an agenda.

Link it up

This section on organising meetings will be important when you attempt the synoptic task in Unit 4.

Working as a receptionist

When you walk into a reception area, you can quickly assess how nice it might be to work in that organisation. A receptionist is usually the first person to greet a visitor, so their behaviour can send a very important message about the organisation as a whole and how it operates.

If you observe the behaviour and **BODY LANGUAGE** of the receptionist and any colleagues you notice walking past the reception desk, you can immediately sense whether or not the organisation operates within a friendly and pleasant atmosphere. This would be important to you if you were sitting in the reception area waiting for a job interview or you were an important visitor bringing new work into the organisation.

There are many duties that a receptionist will need to do. These include:
- managing diaries
- handling mail
- controlling and issuing stationery
- communicating between staff at all levels
- greeting customers and visitors and dealing with their enquiries
- responding to telephone, email and fax enquiries.

What skills do you need to work effectively as a receptionist?

With such a varied role, a receptionist will need to be adaptable, as well as polite, approachable and friendly when dealing with people, especially visitors and customers.

Understanding the organisation's structure

You may think of an organisation's customer as someone who buys the organisation's products or services. This type of customer is known as an external customer. However, you must also consider 'internal' customers.

Examples of internal customers are workplace colleagues or other departments or branches. Even though all internal customers work for the same organisation, they should be offered the same respect and level of service as the organisation's external customers.

A receptionist should have knowledge of the organisation's structure. They should be able to look at an organisational chart, perhaps on the wall, and know at a glance who works in which department and what their name and position is. This is very useful for a new receptionist or perhaps a temporary receptionist.

The chart becomes important when a visitor or telephone caller asks the receptionist who to speak to regarding a particular query. The receptionist will need to know who to transfer the call to.

The receptionist should also have a list of qualified first aiders and their contact details so that they can be contacted quickly if there is an emergency.

Practise

When working as an administrator or receptionist, it is important to use the telephone in a professional manner.

1. Work with a fellow learner to research the important skills that you will need when using a telephone to receive or make calls.

2. Role play a scenario where a customer telephones your organisation to complain about the service they received from a staff member. One of you should play the role of the customer and one of you should play the role of the administrator receiving the call. Put the skills you have researched into practice.

3. Ask for feedback from the rest of the group who have been observing your role play. Identify the steps you need to take to improve your communication skills when using the telephone.

Arranging business trips

When arranging a business trip for a manager or colleague, it's important to make sure that everything has been carefully planned in order to minimise the risk of anything going wrong.

You could start by having a meeting with the person(s) who is going away, to establish:

- when they need to leave and when they intend to return
- where they are going and why
- the type of accommodation they prefer
- what the budget is
- allowable expenses
- who they will be meeting with and when
- the purpose of the trip
- travel arrangements (including tickets, passports or **VISA** requirements)
- insurance cover
- contact arrangements while they are away (for example in an emergency)
- who will cover their usual work commitments while they are away
- briefing notes (to give travellers background information for the trip such as time differences and currency exchange rates)
- cultural, language and social observations and places of interest to visit in their free time.

Making travel and accommodation bookings

When making travel and accommodation bookings, the administrator's role is to ensure the traveller's requirements are fully met. If your traveller is going abroad, you should consider using a reputable travel agent who can work with you to confirm accommodation and travel arrangements. You can telephone a reputable travel agent or visit their website to book and confirm the traveller's requirements. You will need to establish the times of travel and any special requirements, and make sure that you receive tickets in good time. If your traveller has any particular medical requirements, make sure you inform the travel agent when you are making bookings.

If you are arranging a domestic trip, you will need to find out if your organisation uses a car hire company or whether you need to book a suitable car for your traveller. You should contact the hire company and receive confirmation that the booking has been made. Make sure you know when the car can be collected.

Make sure you obtain authorisation from a manager before you book accommodation for your traveller. You may be asked to book a room with a hotel that is used regularly by the organisation. If not, it is a good idea to contact more than one hotel to compare prices and then, with authorisation, contact the selected hotel to check there are vacancies. Ask for confirmation of the booking to be sent to you in writing.

Use of itineraries

When planning a business trip for a colleague, you will need to plan for all possible outcomes. Producing an **ITINERARY** will help you to do this. Figure 2.3 shows how an itinerary could be set out.

Itinerary					
Destination:	New York	**Leave Date:**	3 Dec 20XX	**Return Date:**	5 Dec 20XX
Time	Day one				
6.00 a.m.	Taxi pick-up from home address				
9.30 a.m.	Arrive at Gatwick airport				
11.30 a.m.	Flight departs to New York – Flight number 43224				
2.30 p.m.	Flight arrives at John F Kennedy Airport, New York				
3.00 p.m.	Taxi pick-up from airport to go to Hotel Continental				
4.00 p.m.	Check in to hotel				
Time	Day two				
8.30 a.m.	Meet client representative in hotel foyer for morning coffee				
9.30 a.m.	Meeting in hotel conference room				
12.30 p.m.	Lunch with client in hotel restaurant				

Figure 2.3: Itineraries are useful planning documents

Practise

You have been asked to support the arrangements for a three-day business trip for a colleague who is attending a conference in Belgium.

1. Select three alternative ways to travel from London to Belgium.
2. What bookings would need to be confirmed?
3. What would you need to consider when making these bookings?

Medical and travel insurance cover would need to be arranged for the travellers (your organisation may already have policies in place).

Producing supporting travel documentation

In addition to an itinerary, you should produce a set of briefing notes for your traveller, including all necessary information to ensure their journey is successful. You should attach important documents such as maps, insurance policies, booking reference numbers and emergency contact details to the itinerary you have produced.

If it is an international business trip, include information such as overseas insurance helpline details, business hours and cultural and social observations. If the travel is to a country where English isn't spoken, you could also include useful basic phrases. Don't forget to include medical and passport requirements.

Details of appointments and meetings need to be scheduled in the itinerary. Names of who is being met should also be included.

The consequences of not arranging a business trip effectively could be as follows.

- The traveller misses a vital meeting (the organisation could lose a valuable contract).
- The image and reputation of the organisation is affected.
- A meeting needs to be rearranged (this can be costly, especially if it is overseas).
- A competitor wins the business.
- The allocated budget has been wasted.

Managing information

Your role as an administrator will require you to manage many sources of information on a daily basis. Your organisation is likely to have its own procedures for storing and retrieving information. Filing systems can be paper-based or electronic. Files may be stored in filing cabinets or on a computer.

Storing and retrieving information

Filing procedures should enable you to store, access and distribute information easily and quickly.

Manual filing systems

Files containing information, such as details of customers, will be stored in different ways within different workplaces. There are, for example, different classification systems that administrators can use, such as:

- alphabetical
- numerical
- geographical
- chronological.

If a document is removed from a filing cabinet, an 'Absent' card (or 'Out' card) should be put in its place. This makes it easier to return the file after use.

Also, if a colleague looks for the document while it is in use, the details written on the Absent card will indicate who has the document and when they intend to return it. This helps if there is an unexpected enquiry and the document is needed urgently.

Electronic filing systems

To organise your files electronically, you will need to create folders and subfolders on your computer, as shown in Figure 2.4. In Windows® operating systems, folders can be created by opening a Windows Explorer window and navigating to the location where you wish to create the folder (in the 'Documents' folder or on your computer's desktop, for example). On Apple Mac® operating systems, this is done through the Finder window.

> **Link it up**
>
> Go to Unit 1 for more information on the different types of manual filing system and their uses.

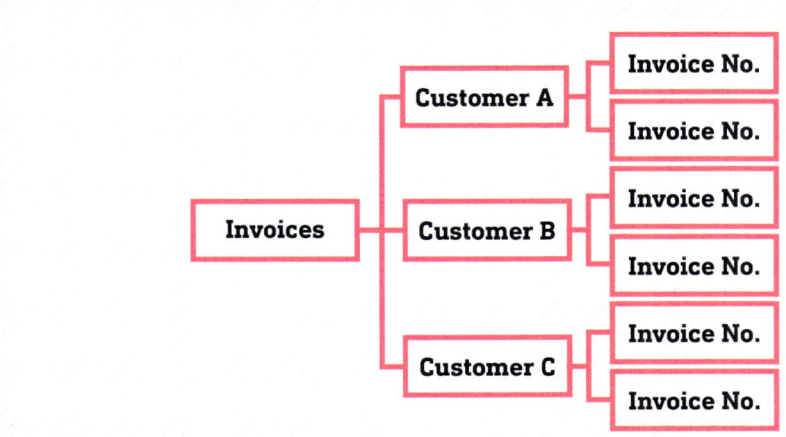

Figure 2.4: An example structure for an electronic filing system

It is important to structure your filing system clearly and logically. For example, within a main folder entitled 'Invoices', you can create subfolders for each customer your organisation deals with. Files are created inside these subfolders where information is stored, including details of when invoices are sent out to customers.

Files contained in folders and subfolders can be sorted by date or alphabetically. This can save time – and frustration – when you need to examine numerous files.

Data input

Familiarise yourself with the manual or electronic filing systems that are used in your organisation. This will help you to use your time more productively when you are inputting data. This speeds up the process of printing documents and distributing them to colleagues who will need them.

When inputting data, you must proofread it to make sure it is accurate and that the grammar and spelling are correct. If you are writing on a manual file, you should make sure your writing is legible to avoid misunderstandings.

Printing, collating and distributing documents

When you print documents you should make sure you follow your organisation's procedures; for example, printing on both sides of the paper and not using colour ink unless it is necessary to do so. As part of your duties you may be required to collate documents and distribute them to the appropriate staff members.

You will need to consider matters of confidentiality when you are printing, collating and distributing files and documents. It is important to follow your organisation's procedures at all times. Never email confidential files without making sure they are password protected. Manual confidential paperwork should be handed to the appropriate person and never left unattended for other people to see.

> **Link it up**
>
> Go to Unit 1 to find more information about the principles of the Data Protection Act 1998. Also go to Unit 3 for information about data management software processes.

A2 Managing time and workload

Time is a very important resource in a business. To help you to manage your own time effectively, you can obtain feedback from experienced colleagues or perhaps from a manager.

Implications of late task completion

It is very important to complete allocated tasks on time; otherwise you may be hindering colleagues from doing their jobs because they are waiting for information from you. Similarly, customers may not receive their goods or services on time, which can lead to complaints. This can affect the organisation's reputation and may result in lost business or compensation claims.

Time management techniques

Tools and techniques to help you manage your time include:

- 'to-do' lists
- **GANTT CHARTS** (a tool that managers can use to measure progress of activities over a period of time)
- manual diaries
- schedules
- electronic diaries
- calendars.

What would you add to a 'to-do' list?

Managing your time well can help you and your colleagues to achieve targets. This in turn will help your department to meet its goals and can contribute to your organisation achieving the business objectives it has in its plan.

Good time management can help you to manage your workload efficiently and avoid stressful situations.

Techniques for managing workload

Some techniques to help you to manage your workload are:
- prioritising tasks according to the situation (routine/non-routine/urgent)
- using a workload plan – you can plan and identify the administrative activities you will need to undertake each day of your working week
- asking colleagues for help
- communicating with your supervisor or managers.

Never be afraid to ask a colleague or a manager for help. This isn't a sign of weakness; instead, it shows that you have a willingness to do things well and in good time.

You shouldn't be surprised if on occasion you find that your work is too challenging or not challenging enough.

If your work is too challenging it can become stressful and could affect your performance, which can affect the rest of your team. If it is not challenging enough, you may become bored and this too will affect your performance. You should always talk to a manager if you feel either scenario is affecting you.

Dealing with distractions

When trying to complete your work tasks in your office you may become distracted from time to time.

This might affect both your ability to enjoy your work and also your time management. Typical workplace distractions are:
- noisy workplace colleagues
- unexpected visitors
- unexpected requests (so you leave an important task in order to deal with them)
- fire alarm practices
- phone calls
- someone telling you to look at social media, instant messaging services, and so on.

Minimising distractions

You must make efforts to 'stay on task'. Some distractions can be politely ignored but sometimes you may have to interrupt your work to deal with distractions (for example, a customer message expecting an immediate response).

Ways to minimise the risks of distractions include the following.
- Turn off your email alerts.
- Turn off mobile phone, PC, social media and instant messaging notifications.
- Use internet-blocking software to help reduce the temptation to shop and browse for personal items while at work (for example, Freedom software).

- Move to a quiet room away from distractions to complete important or urgent tasks.
- Prepare a 'to-do' list and keep to it.

Practise

Produce an A4 poster to display in your workplace that outlines good time management tips.

A3 Completing administrative activities to meet requirements

In your role as an administrator you will be expected to carry out different types of administrative tasks and activities in order to meet the requirements of your organisation.

Although there will be similarities in most organisations, there may be some differences in the activities that you undertake, depending on the size and nature of the organisation that you work in. The focus should be on applying workplace principles – and following procedures – that will enable you to follow what is considered 'best practice'.

Your office manager will make sure you become familiar with your organisation's procedures (you will probably be shown a procedures file) and it is important to carefully follow any instructions that you are given.

Considerations for compliance

Being **COMPLIANT** means that you will be expected to adhere to the rules, regulations, policies and procedures communicated to you by your office manager.

It is also important to listen carefully to what you are being asked to do and it is always a good idea to make a note of instructions as they are given to you. It is easy to forget what was discussed once your manager has walked away.

If you are asked to do something that you are not sure about or do not fully understand, do not be afraid to ask for clarification. Managers and colleagues will prefer you to do this rather than possibly make mistakes because you were not quite sure what you needed to do.

To be able to comply with your organisation's expectations you will need to become familiar with:

- health and safety considerations
- confidentiality
- legislation affecting your business
- the Data Protection Act 1998
- other appropriate/relevant organisation policies.

Link it up

Go to Unit 1 for more general information on the Data Protection Act 1998.

Task briefs

Your manager will take steps to ensure that a task brief given to you is clear and easy to understand. However, it is always useful to spend some time thinking about the skills that you feel you could develop further, such as:

- listening
- note taking
- asking questions
- seeking clarification
- agreeing deadlines.

Task preparation

Before you begin a task, you should plan and prepare in order to avoid distraction later on. Also, you should try not to **PROCRASTINATE** (put off a task until a later time without good reason).

For example, when planning for a stationery stocktake, you will need to collect all of the resources, equipment and information you will need before you start the process. This is better than trying to find the things you need as you progress through the task, which could distract you and slow you down.

Resources required

Equipment needed

Materials necessary

Information needed

Planning equipment and resources needed to complete stocktaking

Practise

Using your school or college's stationery cupboard, carry out a stocktake to identify the number and types of items that are currently available.

Meeting agreed standards

Working towards agreed standards when completing workplace activities will require you to:
- meet agreed timescales
- meet expected quality standards
- meet required levels of accuracy.

Quality-checking work

To assist you with meeting standards, always make sure you check the quality of your work carefully and make any necessary amendments. Communicating effectively with your colleagues and asking for support when necessary can help you with this.

Skills and knowledge check

☐ I understand how health and safety legislation impacts on my role as an administrator.
☐ I can make changes to a colleague's diary as required and communicate these changes to relevant people.
☐ I can prioritise my tasks to make sure I complete everything on time.
☐ When working at reception, I can make and receive telephone calls in a professional manner.
☐ I can use time management tools to help me manage my time effectively.
☐ When I am being given a task, I can make necessary notes and ask questions to clarify understanding.

○ I know what information is needed to send a parcel.
○ I can name the legislation that protects data.
○ I know what essential travel documents need to be prepared for a business trip.
○ I can list the consequences of not meeting deadlines.
○ I can identify distractions and put in place techniques to help reduce these distractions at work.

UNIT 2 | PROVIDING ADMINISTRATIVE SERVICES

B Use office equipment safely and in line with procedures

In this section, you will have the opportunity to learn about the different types of equipment that you will find in an office environment.

The types of equipment used will vary according to the needs of the business, although most organisations have similar types of equipment in their offices. You will need to be able to identify the key features of the equipment used and be aware of what you must consider when operating different types of equipment in an office.

B1 Types of office equipment

In a busy office environment, different types of equipment will be used for a range of purposes. You will benefit from knowing the key features of each piece of equipment.

Categories of equipment

It will be helpful to think about the following categories.

Individual/personal equipment

Each employee may be given specific equipment to operate in their own working area. This could include:

- tablet
- mobile phone
- telephone
- calculator
- memory sticks
- laptop
- PC.

Shared equipment

A team may share equipment that is available to everyone in the office, including:

- printers
- photocopiers
- scanners
- fax machines
- shredders
- **GUILLOTINES** (a tool used to cut paper to size).

When working as an administrator, what day-to-day equipment will you be using?

> **Link it up**
>
> Go to Unit 1 for more information on the purposes of different types of office equipment and factors to consider when using them.

Specialised equipment

Specialist equipment may be used by a limited number of people who have received training to use it. Specialised equipment can include:

- digital projector
- video conferencing software and equipment
- franking machine
- interactive board
- **BINDING MACHINE** (used to make holes in documents so they can be grouped together to form a booklet)
- **LAMINATOR** (used to coat important documents with a protective cover).

Types of office equipment

Imagine that you have been asked to update your department's health and safety procedures manual. To complete this task you might do the following.

- Use the telephone effectively to phone internal customers such as your Health and Safety Officer for advice. You might also speak to external contacts such as a member of the Health and Safety Executive (HSE).
- Use the computer system to create new pages for your manual.
- Use the printer to print off your new pages.
- Photocopy the pages for the spare duplicate manual.
- Scan a document received through the post from the HSE so you can store it electronically for future use.
- Create and laminate a new front cover for the manual to show the date it was updated. You might also use the guillotine to cut the cover to a perfect size.
- Use the document binder to bind all the pages together again (having initially 'undone' the document to carry out this task).
- Use the shredder to shred any confidential information, such as employees' names on the pages you are replacing.

Office equipment features

The main features of different types of office equipment are shown in Table 2.3. Remember that training will be necessary for some equipment!

Table 2.3: Features of office equipment

Equipment	Features	Problems	Resources
Telephone system	• Transfer calls • Put calls on hold • Telephone conferencing	• Needs electricity • Crackling on line or a fault on the telephone line can disrupt a call	• Answering machine • **SOUNDSTATION** (equipment used to project the caller's voice to a group of people)
Computer system	• Communicate with colleagues all over the world • Video chats/conferencing	• Can be hacked • May crash and lose data • Needs Wi-Fi, mobile data or a wired internet connection	• Removable storage media • Camera • Speakers
Printer	• Print documents from screens • Print in colour or black and white • Produce a number of copies	• Out of paper • Paper jam • Needs electricity • May have connection problems if Wi-Fi is connected	• Ink or toner cartridge • Paper • Cleaning kits

Equipment	Features	Problems	Resources
Document scanner	• Duplicate documents onto computer screen • Make changes to scanned documents	• Connectivity issues • Can be slow	• Scanner screen wipes • Cleaning kits
Franking machine	• Cheaper postal service • Allocated postal service to a number of letters	• Can run out of ink • Expensive **CONSUMABLES** (essential items to run a piece of equipment such as ink or toner)	• Ink or toner cartridge • Envelopes • Labels
Laminator	• Provide a clear protective cover • Make documents more durable	• Careless lamination can create bubbles and an uneven surface • Gets very hot during the laminating process	• Various sized laminating pouches
Document binder	• Create a professional finish • Hold important files together as one document	• Misalignment can result in a poor finish • Comb bars can spoil the document finish if incorrect measurements are taken	• **BINDING SPINE COMB BARS** (a machine is used to attach a round spiral length of plastic to a batch of documents to hold them together) • **DURABLE SPINE BARS** (plastic bars that slide over a collection of documents to hold them together) • **BACK BOARDS** (a piece of strong card that is placed at the back of bound documents to provide stability) • **FRONT COVER BOARDS** (a piece of strong card or thick paper that is used as a cover sheet for bound documents)
Shredder	• Destroy confidential documentation	• Can be costly to destroy/remove shredded confidential documentation	• Blade sharpeners • Shredder lubricant sheets or oil • Bags
Guillotine	• Create a professional sharp finish to documentation • Can help to create professional business cards without the expense of getting them printed	• Can be very dangerous: if not used correctly there is a risk of injury such as cuts from the blade, which is very sharp • Misalignment can result in a poor finish	• Blade sharpeners • Replacement cutter heads
Handheld scanner	• A small device to scan barcodes into software • Reduce time from entering barcodes manually	• Limited Wi-Fi range • Battery needs recharging or connection to electricity	• Specialist software

Practise

Produce a list of potential problems that you may encounter when using office equipment. For example, you might think about the dangers of misusing the guillotine.

Training on office equipment is essential to avoid workplace accidents!

Practise

When using office equipment, you must follow the organisation's health and safety procedures to ensure your safety as well as the safety of colleagues.

1 List three potential health and safety problems you might encounter when using a photocopier.
2 Provide solutions to these problems.

B2 Using office equipment

Choosing equipment

Before you choose equipment to use for a task in the office, you should think about:

1. the type of activity you will be doing
2. what is the most suitable item of equipment to use for your activity
3. what will help you to avoid wasting time
4. what is the most cost effective approach.

Types of resources

Different types of resources you may need include:

- printer ink
- toner cartridges
- removable storage media.

It is important that you know how to obtain these resources from the stock room. Remember that there will be procedures to follow and authorisation might be required.

You will need to know what to do if problems occur when you are using equipment, for example, what to do if the printer jams or a photocopier runs out of paper. These problems can cause delays or a backlog of work. You can always ask a colleague or your office manager for guidance, but if you follow procedures or apply the training you have received, you may be able to resolve minor equipment problems yourself.

Working safely with office equipment

Safety when using office equipment is very important. You should:
- follow manufacturers' instructions carefully
- apply the training you have been given
- be fully aware of your organisation's procedures
- know who to contact if you need assistance
- be fully aware of the organisation's health and safety **POLICY** (a document written by managers stating what can or cannot be done within the organisation)
- be familiar with legislation affecting the use of equipment in your organisation, for example, copyright laws.

Minimising waste

Consideration for the environment has received a lot of media attention in recent years. As a result, many groups of **STAKEHOLDERS** (individuals or bodies with an interest in an organisation's activities, such as a bank, government department, customer or supplier) like to know that organisations have sustainability commitments. Taking steps to be environmentally friendly, such as reducing waste, can help to cut costs. This is good for profitability and improves everyone's job security.

CHECKLIST — MINIMISING WASTE

- [ ] Check settings before using equipment
- [ ] Print test pages to check settings
- [ ] Use double-sided photocopies and printouts
- [ ] Turn equipment (and lights) off when not in use
- [ ] Photocopy one document to check its quality before processing a number of copies
- [ ] Reuse scrap paper (not confidential paper)
- [ ] Recycle paper by placing a recycling bin next to printers and photocopiers
- [ ] Encourage colleagues to recycle their waste paper
- [ ] Print in draft mode or eco mode to conserve ink
- [ ] Use recycled paper
- [ ] Use recycled ink cartridges
- [ ] Send messages by email rather than memos
- [ ] Avoid printing emails (unless necessary)

Use recycle bins to reduce waste

Maintaining office equipment

It is important that everyone plays their part in maintaining office equipment. This can prolong the life of the equipment and will ensure that it continues to function properly.

Ways to do this are listed below.
- Replenish consumables.
- Clean equipment after use (in line with procedures, to ensure safety).
- Keep equipment tidy and put items away where they belong.
- Report any faults to the office manager or appropriate person promptly.

You are likely to find labels attached to the electrical equipment in your office indicating the date it was last tested to make sure it is safe to use. Regular maintenance of equipment is important and must be carried out by qualified members of staff or contractors. Regularly maintained equipment will ensure good quality output and safety of users. It is also more environmentally friendly as the equipment will be more efficient, and so will use less energy.

Dealing with equipment failure

If you find a piece of equipment is not working properly, you should take action to resolve the problem. This may be as easy as simply following procedures or reporting the faulty equipment to the appropriate person. Never try to repair an electrical fault or put yourself in danger by attempting to dismantle equipment.

Skills and knowledge check

- [ ] I can deal with problems I may encounter when using office equipment.
- [ ] I can use a range of office equipment.
- [ ] I can follow health and safety procedures when using office equipment.

- ○ I understand the difference between personal, shared and specialised office equipment.
- ○ I understand the key features of different types of office equipment.
- ○ I can identify at least three ways to minimise waste in the office.
- ○ I know why it is important to choose the right equipment in order to complete a task successfully.
- ○ I know where and how to obtain resources.

Practise

Research the three pieces of legislation below and identify how they might impact on you when working in an office:

- Health and Safety at Work Act
- Freedom of Information Act
- Data Protection Act.

UNIT 2 | PROVIDING ADMINISTRATIVE SERVICES

C Demonstrate professional behaviours and effective communication in the work environment

In this section you will learn how demonstrating positive personal behaviours can help you to meet your organisation's expectations. In addition, you will examine the importance of communicating effectively when you find yourself working in different situations.

C1 Professional behaviours

Meeting organisational expectations

As you make efforts to meet the expectations of your managers, it is important that you:
- comply with CODES OF CONDUCT (rules that set out how members of staff are expected to behave in an organisation)
- adhere to health and safety procedures
- follow security procedures
- familiarise yourself with policies and procedures
- support others you work with.

Why is teamwork important?

Following security procedures

Your organisation's managers will take the safety and security of employees and visitors very seriously. In some cases, there will be specific laws that your managers must consider to ensure an appropriate level of security within your organisation. These laws will often form the basis for some of your workplace policies, procedures and codes of conduct.

The consequences of not following security procedures can be very serious. Some typical consequences are shown in Table 2.4.

Table 2.4: Examples and consequences of not following security procedures

Security process	Breach of security processes	Consequences of security processes not being followed properly
Using computer passwords	Letting somebody else use your password	Other people can access your organisation's confidential information.
Shredding confidential documents	Leaving confidential documents on top of the shredding machine to go back and shred later	Confidential information might be read by others, including visitors or contractors.
Signing visitors in and out at reception	Allowing people to enter the building without signing them in or issuing a name badge	People will be unaccounted for in the event of a fire. Also, unauthorised people may be on site which can be a security risk.

Security measures that your managers are likely to have in place include:
- security lights and alarms positioned inside/outside your buildings
- occasional staff searches (including their vehicles)
- lone working policies for those working from home
- password protected systems
- CCTV operations.

Adhering to health and safety procedures

Organisations must follow the Health and Safety at Work Act 1974. One important aspect of this law is that employers must ensure the safety of everyone, including employees, customers or other visitors. Likewise, employees have a duty to take reasonable steps to ensure their own safety as well as that of anyone they interact with in their workplace.

Alongside the Health and Safety at Work Act, there are many other laws and regulations in existence to ensure safety. Your managers will create procedures from these laws, in an effort to prevent accidents and injuries.

Some areas that your managers will need to think about are:
- conducting RISK ASSESSMENTS to identify and control potential hazards
- reducing noise that could affect your hearing
- supplying employees with adjustable office chairs to prevent strain and possible injury
- providing reasonable ventilation so that you can work comfortably
- ensuring a sufficient workspace for each employee, so that you don't feel 'cramped' when working alongside others
- offering training sessions for all staff
- making sure there is temperature control in your office environment
- locating equipment that may release fumes or odour (such as photocopiers) outside your office environment.

As an employee, it is your duty to work closely with your managers and colleagues to ensure your own safety and the safety of everyone you work with and anyone visiting your organisation.

You will need to follow procedures, attend training sessions and know what to do in the event of an emergency.

Steps you can take to follow health and safety procedures include the following.

- Always report accidents and 'near misses' and complete the Accident Book accurately.
- Become familiar with the policies and procedures in your staff handbook (or similar).
- Always follow manufacturers' instructions carefully when working with equipment.
- Never attempt to repair equipment yourself.
- Familiarise yourself with what you must do in the event of an emergency.

Your wellbeing

If you feel stressed for any reason, you should discuss this with a colleague or your office manager. For example, your workload may be too challenging (or not challenging enough) and this may affect the way you feel. If you talk to someone, changes can be made and you will begin to feel better as your stress levels go down.

Demonstrating positive personal behaviours

You probably behave differently when you are out with your friends compared to when you are at work with your colleagues and managers.

In the workplace, you will need to demonstrate positive personal behaviours so that the people you work with will consider you to be a professional person.

You can demonstrate your positive personal behaviour by making efforts to:

- be polite, reliable and trustworthy
- show respect for the values, beliefs and views of others
- show a willingness to work effectively and efficiently
- show a willingness to accept instructions
- adopt a positive approach to work.

To be professional, you must have a positive attitude and avoid negativity

When working in an office environment, from time to time you may hear comments such as 'She is very professional in her approach' or 'He behaved very professionally'. Your colleagues observe each other's behaviours and make assessments accordingly.

It is important to take steps to show that you can behave in a professional manner. Adhering to your organisation's policies, procedures and codes of conduct can help you to operate in an acceptable manner but it is also important to be aware of your personal approach towards your workplace tasks and the way you interact with your colleagues. Making efforts to be polite, courteous and cooperative at all times will help you with this.

Being polite, reliable and trustworthy

If you are polite to your colleagues, visitors and customers you will earn their respect. You will be regarded as somebody who is polite and this will also help you to feel good about yourself and increase your morale.

Similarly, if you show that you can keep promises and carry out your tasks on time, you will earn a reputation as somebody who is trustworthy and reliable.

Showing respect for the values, beliefs and views of others

Everyone 'likes to be liked' and everyone likes to be respected by others they work with. A useful saying to remember is 'Treat others in the way that you would like to be treated yourself.'

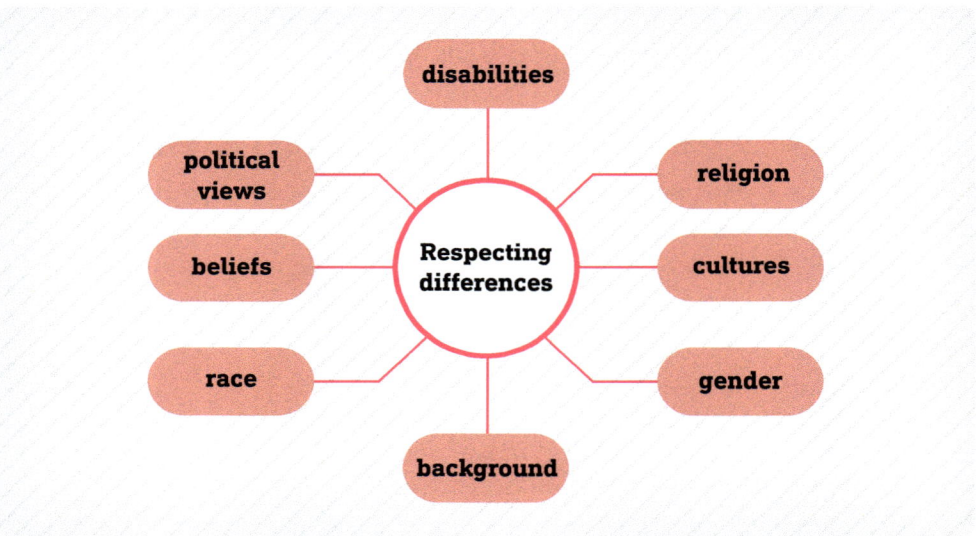

Figure 2.5: Respecting employee differences in the workplace

Understanding that not everyone is the same as you and taking time to consider other people's feelings can, in turn, help you to earn respect. It is also important to have 'self-respect'.

As you make efforts to be respectful to others, they will respect you in return. Mutual respect improves motivation and morale, leading to improved performance and productivity.

Are you respectful? Check whether you are by considering the following.

> **CHECKLIST** | **RESPECTING YOURSELF AND OTHERS**
>
> - [ ] Say 'please' and 'thank you' as appropriate.
> - [ ] Ask yourself whether you could have dealt with a situation in a better or different way.
> - [ ] Be aware of your body language and your **TONE OF VOICE**.
> - [ ] Be aware of your personal appearance.
> - [ ] Only use appropriate humour that won't offend others.
> - [ ] Demonstrate good manners in meetings or when having conversations with others.
> - [ ] Seek permission before using a colleague's equipment or borrowing their stationery.

Willingness to learn and take instructions

When your office manager or another member of staff approaches you with a task, you should show enthusiasm and accept the task willingly. Listen carefully to instructions; if there is anything you are not sure about, do not be afraid to ask for further information. This will show that you are willing to learn and keen to complete the task correctly.

Adopting a positive approach to work

On a daily basis, you can impress your colleagues by showing that you care about the work that you carry out. This will make you feel that you are making progress and your colleagues are likely to value your input and appreciate the work you do. Other ways to show your positivity in work are:

- turning up to work on time
- showing enthusiasm during meetings and other activities
- providing help and support to your colleagues
- dealing efficiently with customers and visitors.

This behaviour will help you to be recognised as a valued member of the team, which in turn can help your future promotion prospects.

C2 Communicating effectively in different work situations

You might find yourself operating in different situations and scenarios during work time. These might be:

- team meetings
- one-to-one meetings
- internal enquiries
- external enquiries.

Verbal and non-verbal communication

It's worth considering how your behaviour might change in different circumstances. Regardless of circumstances, it is always important to remain approachable and professional.

You should also be aware of the way you communicate with colleagues, customers, visitors and managers working at different levels.

How important is effective communication in team meetings?

Verbal communication

Depending on who you are speaking to, your verbal communication may differ in the following ways.

- Tone of voice.
- Volume.
- Whether you speak formally or informally (think about the formality of the language you use).
- How fast or slowly you speak.
- Giving people time to finish their sentences before you respond.
- The language you use, for example, industry-specific terms, JARGON (words that are specific to a profession or group of people that are hard for others to understand), abbreviations.

Verbal communication techniques

It is important that you consider verbal communication techniques, such as the use of relevant and appropriate language within different circumstances. Some of the different verbal communication techniques you could use include:

- **questioning** – it may also be appropriate for you to question anything you're not sure about in order to clarify it. This might be a situation where your manager gives you instructions.
- **active listening** – this is when you need to concentrate and listen carefully without being distracted.
- **reflecting** – it is often useful to reflect upon something that someone has said. By reflecting you can decide if you actually do understand what has been communicated and whether you are doing things in the right way.
- **summarising** – when explaining something you may summarise what you want someone to know. Not everyone will need full details of a process or situation.
- **mirroring** – this involves discreetly copying somebody's behaviour or mannerisms, in order to put them at ease and build trust between you and that person. An example of mirroring is lowering your tone of voice when speaking with a quiet or timid member of staff.

Non-verbal communication

In the workplace, it is useful to be aware of other people's body language. For example, in a meeting the chairperson may be able to tell how people are feeling just by looking at their body language. If someone is yawning, they may simply be tired but they might be bored. In response, the chairperson should 'read' this body language and try to make the meeting more interesting.

Written communication

When communicating through writing, things to consider are:
- how formal or informal the message should be
- whether to use a company standard template
- email and letter etiquette
- accuracy of content
- clarity of the message
- CORPORATE BRANDING (promoting the reputation and image of an organisation, for example, by using a company logo that will become recognised by CONSUMERS over a period of time)
- layout and format
- grammar and spelling (proofreading).

> **Practise**
>
> You have received a message from a colleague asking for confirmation that arrangements have been made for her business trip to Paris at the end of the month. Respond to this message.
>
> In your response you should inform her of what you have arranged in preparation for her business trip, including travel and accommodation arrangements.
>
> Make sure you follow your organisation's procedures for writing emails.

Types of communication

✔	Verbal communication	✔	Written communication	✔	Non-verbal communication
	FACE-TO-FACE		Letters		Crossed arms
	Telephone		Emails		Frowning
	Teleconferencing		Notes		Smiling
	Voicemail		Texts		Looking confused
	Video conferencing		Taking orders		Using hand gestures
	Seminars		Memos		Eye contact
	Interviews		Posters		Touching
	Presentations		Agendas		Posture
	Meetings		Newsletters		Shaking hands
			Suggestion boxes		
			Noticeboard information		
			Invitations		
			Financial reports		

Figure 2.6: There are many different types of communication to consider

Link it up

For more information on effective communication when working as part of a team, go to Unit 1 on how working relationships contribute to an effective business.

Planning communication

You can become better at communicating by thinking about the following questions.
- Are you communicating with internal or external customers?
- What is the purpose and reason for your communication?
- What is the best format to use?
- What is the best time to communicate?
- How formal should the communication be?

Communication is about getting the right message to the right people at the right time – and in the most effective way. You should welcome any feedback you receive and use it constructively to improve your performance in the workplace.

Practise

When communicating with colleagues, managers and other stakeholders, you must be aware of your body language.

Write down examples of body language that shows:

1 someone's interest in something
2 someone's lack of interest in something.

Skills and knowledge check

- [ ] I can outline how you should set out and produce a range of organisational documents.
- [ ] I can demonstrate positive behaviours when speaking with colleagues and other stakeholders.
- [ ] I can demonstrate 'active listening'.

○ I know the difference between a policy and a procedure.
○ I know it is vital to check the quality of my work.
○ I understand the importance of following an organisation's code of conduct and meeting the organisation's expectations.
○ I understand the importance of being aware of my body language when talking to people.

Ready for assessment

Your office manager has asked you to provide cover for the receptionist, who will be on holiday for two weeks. You will be able to ask your colleagues and your office manager for guidance and assistance as you take on this role. You will be expected to work to the best of your ability on a daily basis.

The receptionist has left notes to assist you with the tasks you will need to complete. You will have access to his manual desk diary and you also have access to your other colleagues' electronic diaries. Complete the following tasks.

- Plan and prepare documentation for the next team meeting, including an agenda and an attendance list.
- Create an itinerary for a colleague who is attending a business conference.
- Design and prepare a leaflet for staff that identifies potential problems when using a photocopier and explain how to overcome them.
- Produce a short presentation using appropriate software such as Microsoft PowerPoint®. A colleague has asked you to prepare six slides that she can use in a staff training session entitled 'Demonstrating positive personal behaviours'.

WORK FOCUS

HANDS ON

Below are some actions that you should undertake and some that you shouldn't, as you develop your skills further.

Skills	Do	Don't
Handling mail	Sort external mail by postage type	Open private or confidential mail
	Distribute internal mail on time	Open suspicious letters or packages
Managing diaries	Learn how to use manual and electronic diaries	Make changes in a diary without agreeing them with relevant people
	Enter clear and sufficient details in diaries	Agree to appointments without checking other priorities
Supporting meetings	Take into consideration special needs of delegates who may be attending	Forget to check that equipment such as projectors will work
	Send out notice of meeting and invitations in good time	Forget to assess the room for suitability
Making and receiving telephone calls	Be polite	Chew gum when talking with others
	Smile when talking on the phone	Allow yourself to be distracted
	Let the caller know when you are placing them on hold or transferring the call	Talk fast
	Take notes of callers' details	
Making travel and accommodation arrangements	Confirm arrangements with the traveller	Forget to take into consideration the special requirements of the traveller
	Check travel insurance cover	Book the most expensive mode of transport
Greeting and looking after visitors	Greet with a smile	Let a visitor see a colleague without a prior appointment
	Listen to visitors' requirements carefully	
	Communicate clearly	Leave confidential documents visible at reception
Operating office equipment safely	Follow procedures and read manufacturers' instructions carefully	Try to repair electrical equipment yourself
	Be aware of health and safety procedures	Attempt to move heavy office equipment
	Tidy up after using equipment to help prevent accidents	

UNIT 2 | PROVIDING ADMINISTRATIVE SERVICES

Ready for work?

When working as an administrator there are some very important skills that you will need to develop so that you portray a professional image.

The quiz below will help you to identify whether you are displaying professional behaviours when you are in your work environment.

Tick all the answers that you think are correct (more than one answer may be correct).

1 When working with others you should:
- [ ] A be polite
- [ ] B take a long lunch break
- [ ] C listen carefully
- [ ] D turn up late to meetings

2 When communicating with colleagues or visitors you should:
- [ ] A take notes when receiving telephone calls
- [ ] B be aware of your body language
- [ ] C keep visitors waiting at reception
- [ ] D proofread your work

3 When solving problems, you should:
- [ ] A get clarification from your manager
- [ ] B never refer to the manufacturers' instructions
- [ ] C get feedback from your colleagues
- [ ] D refer to your organisation's procedures

4 When you are preparing for work tasks you should:
- [ ] A make sure you understand what you need to do
- [ ] B ignore health and safety procedures
- [ ] C gather together all of your equipment and resources
- [ ] D never ask for help

Answers: 1 A, C; 2 A, B, D; 3 A, C, D; 4 A, C

87

3 Using Business Technology to Process and Communicate Information

Can you imagine not having a computer, smartphone or tablet for a day? What would you do? How would this affect your work and personal life? We rely heavily on technology for all sorts of things these days and it is important to understand how we use technology for business.

In this unit, you will learn about a range of business technologies. This includes web-based technology such as social media, shared drive workspaces and the Internet, which we use to communicate and share information at work. You will also develop skills to select the most appropriate equipment, technology and applications software to produce different business documents.

How will I be assessed?

The assessment for this unit is a practical activity, set in a realistic scenario, and will draw on what you will learn in this unit. You will be taught how to produce business information using data management software, how to produce business documents using the most appropriate software applications and how to use web-based technology to communicate and share information. You will also be involved in some practical activities to help apply your knowledge and understanding before taking the assessment.

Assessment criteria

Pass	Merit	Distinction
Learning aim A: Process business information accurately using data management software		
A.P1 Use computer equipment in line with health, safety and security procedures. **A.P2** Enter, edit, format and store information accurately using data management software appropriate to the requirements of tasks.	**A.M1** Use basic software interrogation tools to correctly extract and collate information to meet task requirements.	**A.D1** Demonstrate navigation and use of more advanced interrogation tools to analyse, manipulate and present accurate business information to meet task requirements.
Learning aim B: Produce fit-for-purpose business documents using applications software		
B.P3 Select and use the appropriate applications software to meet the requirements of the task. **B.P4** Use basic software tools to edit and format business documents that meet given requirements and acceptable business standards.	**B.M2** Use a range of software tools and techniques to format, structure and finish business documents that meet given requirements and acceptable business standards.	**B.D2** Use more advanced software tools and techniques to design, structure and finish business documents that meet given requirements and acceptable business standards.
Learning aim C: Use web-based technology to communicate and share information		
C.P5 Follow guidance in using web-based technology tools to communicate information in line with given requirements and business standards. **C.P6** Follow guidance in using web-based technology tools to share information in line with given requirements and business standards.	**C.M3** Select and use the appropriate web-based technology competently to communicate and share information in line with given requirements and business standards.	**C.D3** Critically review own practices in using web-based technology to communicate and share business information, identifying opportunities for future improvements.

A Process business information accurately using data management software

In business, we rely on computers to manage and communicate information. Technology has evolved significantly, having a major impact on the way businesses operate.

A1 Types of business technology

Administrators use different computing devices (such as tablets, laptops and smartphones) and hardware to access a range of software and system applications in the office or remotely from different locations. By using ONLINE BUSINESS TECHNOLOGY, organisations can reach more people and potential customers in a more effective and efficient way.

Range of online business technology

We can use online business technology to carry out business activities such as conferencing, reviewing documents online, research, networking, marketing and sales. Examples of web-based technology systems include social networks, video conferencing and shared workspaces.

Social networking

SOCIAL NETWORKS are websites that allow users to communicate with each other. As an administrator you can interact with other users to sell your organisation's products or services, share images, videos and new product details to engage with your audience, and offer quality customer service.

Video conferencing

Some staff work remotely and there may be times when you need to bring people together to discuss projects or other work-related issues. An ideal way is to use VIDEO CONFERENCING facilities such as Skype™.

> **Link it up**
> For more on social media, go to section C1, 'Social media', later in this unit.

> **Link it up**
> To find out more about using video conferencing, go to section C1, 'Video conferencing', later in this unit

What are the advantages of video conferencing?

Video conferencing uses computers with webcams to provide a video link between two or more people. They are able to see and talk to one another, and often **SHARE SCREENS**. Screen sharing allows a member in the video conference to show other members an open document or window on their screen.

Shared workspaces

Not all employees work in the same office, so **SHARED WORKSPACES** allow people in different locations to access and share files online and work collaboratively on business activities.

Examples of online shared workspaces include:
- SharePoint® – useful for storing and accessing documents and information from anywhere (either internally or externally)
- Dropbox™ – useful for storing and sharing files remotely
- Google Docs™ – useful for working on documents collaboratively in real time
- Instant messaging – useful for sending and reading messages online in real time.

Different types of computing devices

Some administrators working in an office use a desktop computer or a laptop. However, not all business activities take place in the office. Sometimes people work from home or 'on the go' so the range of computing devices must accommodate this.

- Desktop computer – a personal computer that is designed to stay in one location and fits on a desk. It usually consists of a monitor, a keyboard, a mouse and a horizontal or vertical tower containing the processor.
- Tablet – a portable device with touchscreen facilities. Sometimes a separate keyboard can be attached if necessary. Tablets are typically smaller than a laptop but larger than a smartphone. They can be used anywhere, although some of the applications may require access to the Internet. Cases are often used to protect the screen from damage.
- Laptop – a portable device and personal computer. Laptops can be used temporarily in different locations to complete business activities such as checking emails, working online or producing and editing documents. These are ideal if you need to work away from the office.
- Smartphone – a portable device smaller than a tablet. It is used for making and receiving phone calls, sending and receiving messages and accessing the Internet and emails. Some companies use smartphones for daily business activities.

Types of computing hardware

In addition to the computing devices already mentioned, there is a range of other **HARDWARE**, i.e. the physical parts or components of a computer system, that you may need to perform your business activities. As well as the external parts and equipment, there are internal parts, such as the motherboard, central processing unit and hard drive. You will need to use different equipment depending on the situation, as Table 3.1 shows.

Table 3.1: Computing hardware

Hardware type	Description
Visual display unit (VDU)	This is the monitor or computer screen and allows you to view your work. VDUs come in different sizes and resolutions which affect the quality of the display.
Keyboard	Enables you to input information into the computer. Keyboards can be separate or built in to the portable device.
Printer	Allows you to print out business documents. Printers can be wired or used wirelessly. Several devices can print to the same printer. Printouts are available in different colour options and sizes (e.g. A5, A4, A3). Some printers have scanning and copying facilities.
Mouse	This is an input device and can be used with a personal computer or portable device to select a specific location on the screen. They are available in wired or wireless options and need to be used on a flat surface.
Scanner	A scanner is a device that copies documents and converts them into electronic files. Scanners capture images from photographs, business documents, magazines, books, leaflets and posters using a laser.

Types of computer software

In order for the hardware to carry out the computing functions required, such as producing documents, accessing the Internet and storing information, it needs **SOFTWARE**. Software is a collection of instructions for computer programs that allows you to operate the device and related hardware, and to perform computing tasks.

Systems software

SYSTEMS SOFTWARE includes programs that manage the computer itself, such as the **OPERATING SYSTEM**, which manages the basic functions of a computer. System software acts as an interface between the applications software, the user and the computer hardware. The programs work in the background to manage the overall resources and operations of the computer (see Figure 3.1).

As an administrator, you may need to make use of these programs to:
- tell the computer what to do and which applications or software to open
- perform basic maintenance to help the computer to run more efficiently or securely
- check where files are stored on the computer
- check how much storage space is left on the computer or device
- delete files
- check for computer viruses
- **BACK UP** data.

UNIT 3 | USING BUSINESS TECHNOLOGY TO PROCESS AND COMMUNICATE INFORMATION

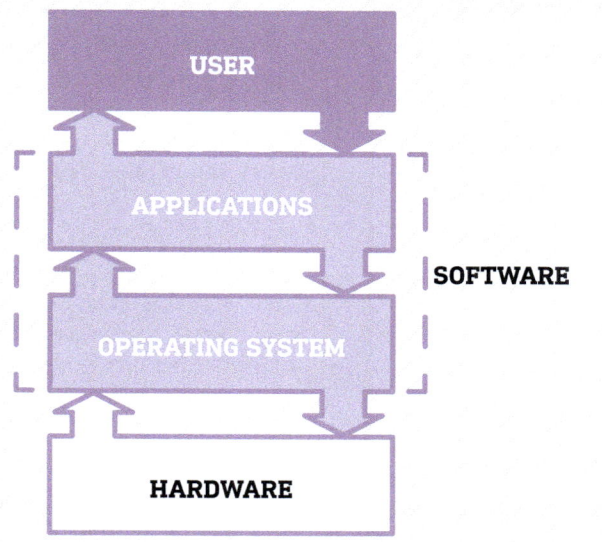

Figure 3.1: The relationship between hardware and software

Applications software

Applications software is the computer programs that administrators use to perform their business tasks. Software has been developed for all kinds of business use, such as creating, viewing and editing documents, spreadsheets, presentations, images and other media files. Applications software works across the different operating systems on your desktop, laptop, tablet and smartphone.

> **Practise**
>
> 1 Make a list of the eight applications you use most often.
> 2 Compare your list with a partner to see how many you have in common.
> 3 Which of these applications do you think you would use as an administrator?

Examples of business software include those shown in Table 3.2 on page 94.

It is important to select the most appropriate software for the business document you intend to produce

Table 3.2: Business software

Business application software	Uses
Word-processing (e.g. Word®) Word files have .docx as the current file extension	Create business documents such as letters, forms, leaflets and posters. Add text, tables and images. The mail merge feature allows you to create a standard letter and personalise it for many individuals.
Spreadsheets (e.g. Excel®) Excel files have .xslx as the current file extension	Add text and numbers to create sales forecasts, stock analysis and product lists. Spreadsheets also allow you to do automated calculations. Information can be converted into graphs and charts.
Data management (e.g. Access®) Access files have .accdb as the current file extension	Store, organise, analyse and manage large amounts of data such as customer or patient records. Once information is inputted, you can sort the data or retrieve specific information such as sales figures for a certain month.
Presentations (e.g. PowerPoint®) PowerPoint files have .pptx as the current file extension	Prepare slides for a verbal presentation during a meeting or event. Slides can contain text or images with links to audio and video files.
Desktop publishing (e.g. iStudio Publisher®) iStudio Publisher files have .ispx as the current file extension	Create more advanced and professional layouts and documents such as newspapers, magazines and newsletters. You can also design letterheads, business cards, templates and brochures.

System applications

An application is a program that runs on a computer. System applications are what you see and use on a computer such as operating systems, local applications and web-based applications.

Operating systems

These applications operate the computer. The three most common operating systems are:

- Microsoft Windows®
- Mac OS®
- Linux®

Each operating system has a different look and feel to it, although the basic principles are the same and are designed to be easy to use. It is important for administrators to know how to use these systems correctly to conduct their business activities.

For tablets and smartphones, there are different operating systems designed for use with mobile devices. Examples of these are Apple iOS and Google Android™.

Local applications

Local applications are those applications that are installed on your own computer or device, such as security or antivirus software. You will see them on the desktop or menus.

UNIT 3 | USING BUSINESS TECHNOLOGY TO PROCESS AND COMMUNICATE INFORMATION

All of the icons in this menu relate to different local applications

Web-based applications

Web-based applications are applications that can be accessed anywhere and from any device with an Internet connection. These applications require a web browser to function such as Internet Explorer, Google Chrome™ and Safari®.

Examples of web-based applications include:

- websites (for example, www.google.co.uk) – used to research and share information
- webmail (for example, Yahoo! Mail, Gmail™, Hotmail) – used to read and send emails through your browser and web-based account
- instant messaging (for example, Messenger, Jabber, WhatsApp) – used to send messages instantly. Organisations use instant messaging to talk to customers directly by text rather than by phone
- collaborative working tools (for example, Google Docs™, Huddle, SharePoint®) – used when people need to work together on a document in real time.

Practise

1. Check the device you are currently using. What is the name of its operating system?

2. You have been asked to carry out the following business activities. List the technology that you would use for each:

   a) creating an electronic telephone directory of all staff for use internally

   b) providing updated information about a new product to five regional managers

   c) marketing the new product to customers online

   d) researching a new topic

   e) working collaboratively on a new document.

95

A2 How business technology systems support organisations

Systems and software applications allow you to operate much more effectively and efficiently at work and to produce documents that look professional. As a business administrator it is important that you are aware of different technology and its uses in the workplace.

Organisational uses of business technology

In the office, business technology supports organisations in a number of ways to produce documents, store information, process data and communicate with customers and staff.

Document production

Documents are produced to convey information to staff, potential customers and the general public. As an administrator, you can take advantage of the different software applications to produce a document that is fit-for-purpose. Examples of business documents and software application tools or features that are often used to communicate information are shown in Table 3.3.

Table 3.3: Business documents and software application tools or features and their uses

Document	Use
Report	Provide text or graphical information for a specific purpose
Letter	Send formal or informal information to staff and customers
AGENDA	Provide a list of topics to be discussed during a meeting
Meeting **MINUTES**	Provide a formal record of the attendees, discussions and outcomes of a meeting
Spreadsheet	Provide statistical or analytical data in text/numerical format
Slideshow presentation	Present text, graphics, audio and video files during a meeting
Software application tool or feature	**Use**
Mail merge	Send personalised letters to many individuals
Graphs and charts	Provide statistical or analytical data using a visual format
Database	Store information and compare or contrast data or trends

Information storage

Organisations store information about their staff, products and competitors to retrieve and use at a later date. They keep personnel records and store documents they have created, such as records of sales and competitor prices. Some documents may be in paper format but most information is stored digitally, either on a local application (on a computer hard drive) or by using a web-based application.

Data processing

Administrators can use technology to process data. Data may need to be inputted to a spreadsheet or database, for example details of a new member of staff joining the company or payroll information. You may need to edit details in an existing document, such as a staff change of address or product price increase.

Communicating with customers and staff

Administrators can use business technology in a variety of ways to communicate with their customers and staff. Information can be sent to staff by email, letter, newsletters or through updates on the company intranet. As an administrator, you will need to know how formal or informal the **COMMUNICATION** needs to be and the best way to share it with your audience.

Communication with customers is two-way. Some examples of how organisations can communicate with their customers using technology include:

- customer updates – customers can sign up for updates on products or services that are relevant to them and receive updates via email adverts or newsletters
- customer responses – a quick and easy way for customers to get answers to questions is via text message; their responses could feed into a database and be analysed
- customer feedback – services such as SurveyMonkey are examples of online surveys and questionnaires which can be used to get vital customer feedback (polls can also be effective tools)
- customer complaints – these can be received via letter, in person, or as posts on the organisation's social media page; customer complaints need to be managed carefully.

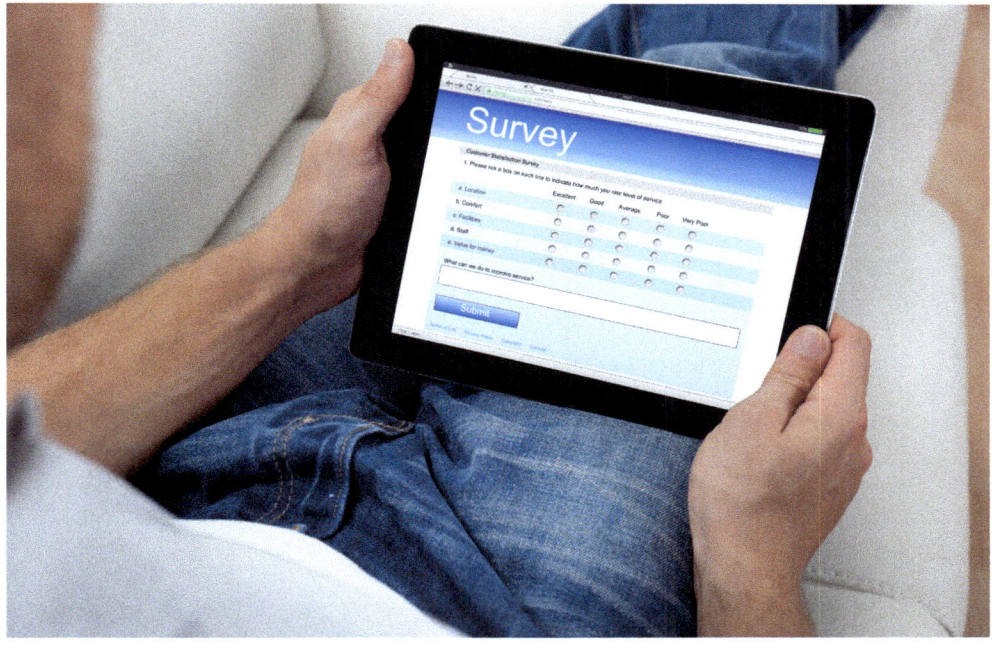

Customer feedback is vital to the success of the business and for developing new products and services

Benefits of using business technology

Using technology in business can provide benefits to organisations and their customers. It is important that systems are easy to use and that information can be processed swiftly and correctly.

Automated processing of information

An automated system can recognise whether a customer is a repeat customer and will populate forms with essential data such as name and address and some payment details. Automated systems can generate other documents such as invoices, remittance forms or returns forms. These systems are particularly useful for online sales and banking.

Speed of processing

Using technology helps organisations to process information quickly. Some systems enable customers to log in using their email addresses or social media accounts to save them having to repeat essential data.

Systems can handle large amounts of data by using databases to record customer details and their orders. Sales can be turned around at the click of a few buttons to make the customer experience as easy as possible.

Secure storage of information

Organisations must follow data management requirements. Systems must be secure to handle personal data such as dates of birth, names, addresses and payment details. Information must be **ACCURATE** and stored in accordance with the organisation's **POLICY**.

Different types of resources for business technology systems

When using business technology systems, it is important that you have all your equipment and resources available when you need them. Some items may be available in-house (such as printer paper) but others may need to be ordered which can take time. Some examples of equipment and resources that may be needed to perform business activities include:

- computer accessories – keyboard, mouse, cables, plugs, routers, webcams, headsets, microphones, USB sticks (memory sticks), disk drives, external hard drives
- consumables – toner cartridges, CDs, pens
- stationery – company letter heads, compliment slips.

Practise

1. Write an email to several customers informing them of a new product launch.
2. What are the advantages of using email as a method of communication rather than post or advertising in a shop window?

Complying with regulatory requirements, standards and safety considerations

Administrators must work safely and comply with legislation, regulations and standards when using technology to process and communicate information. They must cooperate with other members of staff in the organisation to make sure their equipment and workstations are safe to use. Administrators must also follow **PROCEDURES** relating to information security and confidentiality. They must use acceptable behaviours when using web-based technology and comply with business standards or etiquette when producing business documents (see Figure 3.2).

UNIT 3 | USING BUSINESS TECHNOLOGY TO PROCESS AND COMMUNICATE INFORMATION

Figure 3.2: Why is it important to follow the law?

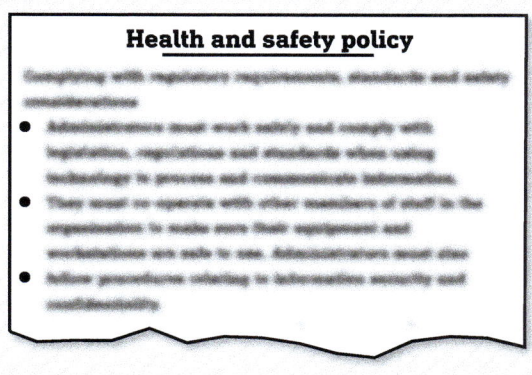

Figure 3.3: Know your company's policies and procedures relevant to your work

It is important to recognise and understand the relevant legislation, regulations and standards including:

- Health and Safety at Work Act 1974
- Computer Misuse Act 1990
- Health and Safety (Display Screen Equipment) Regulations 1992
- Data Protection Act 1998
- Freedom of Information Act 2000
- Privacy and Electronic Communications Regulations 2003
- Equality Act 2010.

Link it up

Go to Unit 1 to find more information on each of the Acts listed here and on the importance of legislation relating to the use, security and storage of information.

Practise

1. How can you make sure you comply with the regulations and legislation listed above when working with a computer?
2. Why is it important that staff understand that they have a duty of care both under law and to their customers?
3. What can organisations do to ensure the staff understand their legal obligations and follow their policies and procedures?

Employers also provide details of accepted behaviours that administrators should adopt when using web-based technology and the quality standards expected when they produce business documents. It is usual practice for staff to be asked not to access websites blocked by the organisation or post personal comments on the organisation's social media. Staff will also be asked not to **DISCLOSE** their business usernames/passwords or controversial or confidential information about the company in the public domain.

A3 Using data management software to process information

Before you communicate information or produce business documentation, you need to process the information that you have been asked for. In order to do this, you may need to ask yourself the following questions.

- How should I collect the information from various sources?
- Where can I access the specific information and files required?
- Which device and software are the most appropriate to process the information?
- What access do I have to different applications software for producing and communicating the business document?
- Which applications software is the most appropriate and how will I use it?

How to access files

To use your computer at work, you will need to follow the organisation's login procedures. You will be given a username and password, which you must not disclose to unauthorised people.

Familiarise yourself with standard features when starting up your computer, such as your desktop icons, the lock-screen function, how to change personal settings and also how to close down your computer. If you notice anything different or suspicious, report this to your manager or the technical team.

If you store a file on the computer, you should know where and how to find it again. This is often called 'housekeeping'. You may need to create folders or sub-folders for your work and store them on your own workspace or shared drive. Devices also have a 'search' function to locate files.

Make sure you have the authority to access specific files. Some documents may be password protected to prevent unauthorised access or may only be accessed by certain members of the organisation (e.g. managers). As an administrator, you must make sure you follow organisational procedures to be safe and secure when using your work computer.

> **Link it up**
>
> Go to Unit 1 to find more information about using different types of office equipment. You will also find more information on how to resolve problems when using office equipment.

Choice and use of input device

There are a number of devices you can use to input data into your computer. These include:

- keyboard – for inputting text, numbers and special characters
- scanner – for taking an electronic image of a document or photograph
- camera – for uploading photos and videos
- voice recognition technology (for example, microphone) – for recording audio.

Collecting information from different sources for data input

When preparing business documents, you will need to extract information from different sources. For example, you may be collating feedback from your customers on their experiences of buying your products or using your services. It is important to make sure you use the information as it was intended and maintain confidentiality of customer details.

It is a good idea to set up a new folder for each piece of work that you have been asked to complete. Collate all your customer information in one place so you can find it again easily and so the original source material can be acknowledged and checked if necessary.

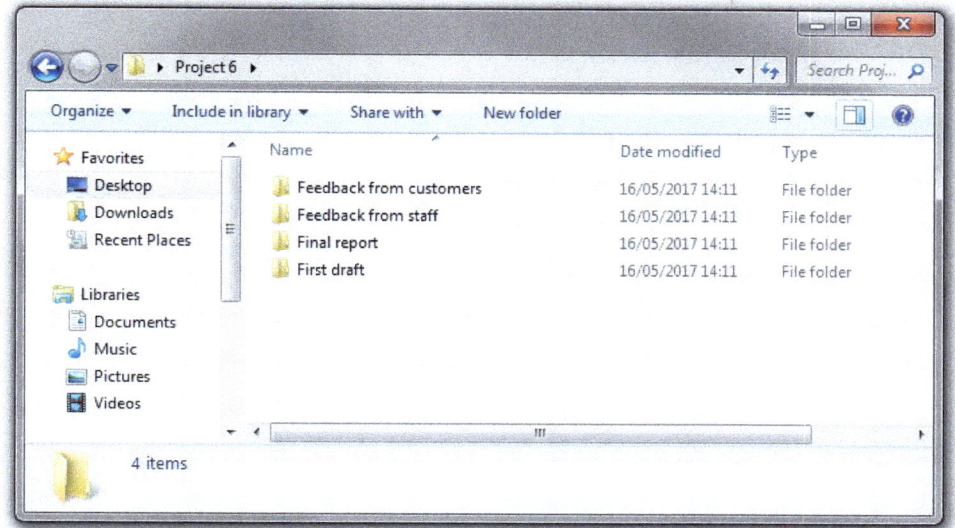

Set up sub-folders so you can find specific documents more easily

You may be collecting information from your colleagues. Documents and emails that they have sent to you can be stored easily in a sub-folder ready for use.

You may use information from databases or spreadsheets, or even from the Internet. Always make a note of your sources and files that you have used so you can refer to them again if necessary.

Using spreadsheet and database software

Spreadsheets and databases have capabilities and functions to allow you to input, process and analyse data that is relevant to the task you have been asked to do. Each application has its own strengths and helps companies to organise and manipulate data.

Administrators need to know how to enter numerical and non-numerical information and edit and save the information or records correctly using suitable software.

Before you start your task, make sure you have a clear understanding of the requirements, how you will go about the task, the system and applications software you will use and the analysis and reporting required.

Spreadsheets

A spreadsheet is used to keep track of data and do calculations while a database is used to store information to be manipulated later. Spreadsheets are used for:

- entering numerical and non-numerical information
- making calculations
- creating graphs and charts
- analysing and manipulating information
- data validation
- producing reports, graphs and charts.

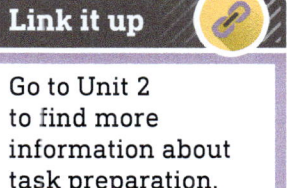

Link it up

Go to Unit 2 to find more information about task preparation, managing your time and workloads.

Databases

Information may start out as a spreadsheet but as the amount of information grows, the need for a database might arise. Databases are used for:

- entering and editing data records
- running database queries
- producing database reports
- holding vast quantities of data.

Companies may use powerful and well-known applications software (such as Microsoft Access®) to store vast quantities of data or they may have their own bespoke software that meets the requirements of the company.

Spreadsheet and database software have different tools and it is important that you know how to use the functions of the software, as shown in Table 3.4.

Table 3.4: Spreadsheet and database tools

Spreadsheet	Database
Entering and editing data	Entering and editing data
Cell alignment and formatting	Selecting and using data queries to filter required data
Number formatting	Viewing queries and reports
Entering formulae	Creating new queries and reports
Sorting and filtering	Formatting tables and reports
Inserting and deleting rows and columns	Designing forms
Freezing and hiding rows and columns	Presenting data
Combining and linking data and worksheets	Changing field type and size, field parameters and formatting fields

How to check records

Information needs to be entered carefully and checked for accuracy, completeness and **VALIDITY** (whether it is genuine or authentic and legally acceptable). Otherwise the data and resulting queries or reports will be unreliable.

- Accuracy – you must check the sources of information and check the dates to confirm the credibility and reliability of information. You also need to check the information to make sure it matches the specified requirements; otherwise time will be wasted in repeating the task.
- Completeness – you should check for completeness. For example, if you had been inputting data from a survey and some people had not completed some questions, this would affect the statistical analysis.
- Validity – you can run validity checks on both spreadsheets and databases. Validation is an automatic computer check on the data entered to make sure it is sensible and reasonable. It does not check the accuracy of the data. Examples of validation checks include:
    - presence check – checks data has been entered and not left blank
    - look up table – checks acceptable values in a table and allows only certain data to be entered (e.g. a shop may include specific sizes of clothing – 8, 10, 12, 14, etc.)
    - format check – checks the data is in the right format (e.g. dates, postcodes).

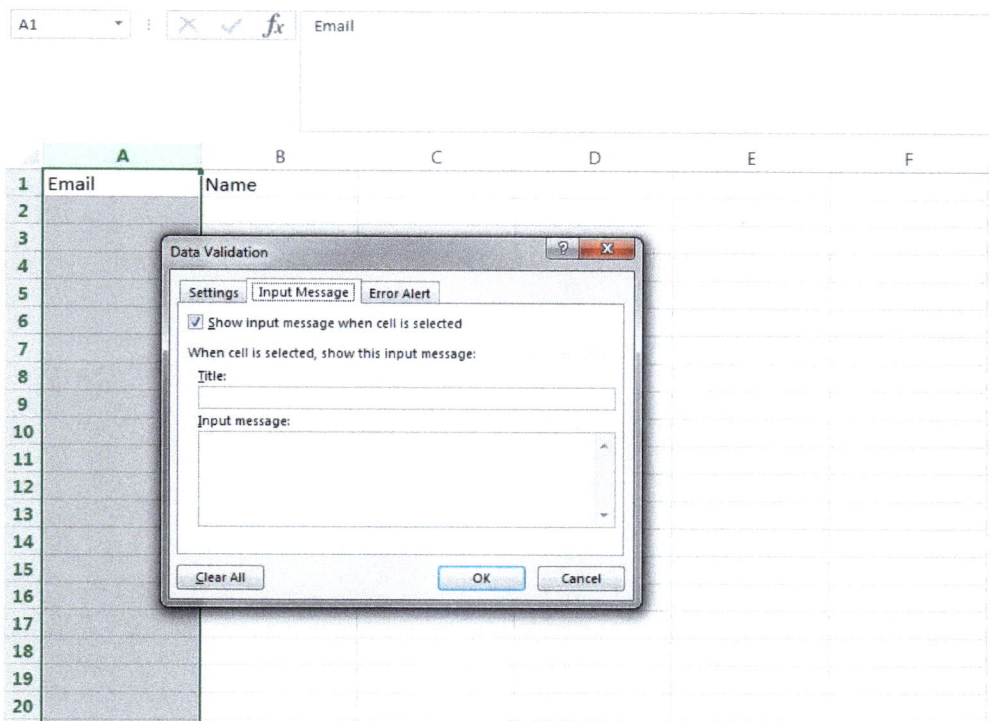

The Data Validation feature helps you to control what can be entered in your worksheet

Practise

You work for a new bakery store and your manager has asked you to set up a spreadsheet to track the sales of its products.

1. Enter the details of six bakery products.
2. Enter details for their sales for January, February and March.
3. Check your data for accuracy.
4. Validate your entries.
5. Prepare a bar chart to compare the sales figures.
6. At what point would the company need to consider creating a database for this information?

Responding appropriately to any problems in using software

Things don't always go to plan and sometimes you may need help with original source material, calculations or validation queries.

It is important that you check your work in the first instance to make sure that you have not overlooked something obvious. If you cannot resolve the problem, or there is an IT issue, then bring this to the attention of a team member who may be able to help you.

Storing files

You may be dealing with new or existing files when processing data. It is important that you store information correctly at all times. You may need to simply save a file or save a copy of a file, in a different format or to a different location.

When saving a file, give the file a meaningful name. Remember, this needs to be professional and must mean something to other people, especially if it is a shared file.

Always save your work regularly to avoid losing essential information, particularly if you are dealing with large amounts of data, images, tables and so on. When saving your work, file extensions are also important. These come after the filename and tell you which icon or application software to use to open that particular file. Examples are .xlsx, .pptx, .jpg, .mp4, .mov.

When working with other colleagues or customers, it is important to make sure that your file is supported by older versions of the applications software or different operating systems.

Work as a team to make sure everyone can open the document correctly and contribute to it if required

Practise

Look at the files you already have stored on your computer. Are the filenames meaningful? Could they be better organised? Do you need to delete any files you no longer need to free up some storage?

Before closing down any application software, save and close any records and files correctly to avoid losing essential information.

Skills and knowledge check

☐ I can confidently check the accuracy of source data.
☐ I can list three capabilities of database software and three capabilities of spreadsheet software.
☐ I can discuss the difference between word-processing and desktop publishing applications software.
☐ I am confident I could comply with the Data Protection Act.
☐ I have practised processing and analysing a variety of data using different applications software.

○ I can identify three examples of computer hardware.
○ I know what is meant by system applications.
○ I know why it's important not to give out my username and password.
○ I know how to store files appropriately.

Link it up

Go to Unit 1 to find more information about saving and storing business documents.

UNIT 3 | USING BUSINESS TECHNOLOGY TO PROCESS AND COMMUNICATE INFORMATION

B Produce fit-for-purpose business documents using applications software

In order to communicate information, you first need to process the information and design documents that are appropriate to the reader.

B1 Types of business documents and their uses

In business, you often need to produce documents to share or present information, record outcomes of meetings or communicate with colleagues and customers. See Figure 3.4 for points to consider when planning to produce a business document.

Some organisations use a template for their documents. Typical business documents include letters, reports, meeting minutes, agendas, presentation slideshows, leaflets and flyers.

B2 Planning and producing business documents using applications software

Figure 3.4: It may be helpful to create a list of things to keep in mind before you start

What would happen if you sent a document to a customer without having planned it out carefully or checked the contents for accuracy? What effect would this have on the business? It is important for administrators to invest time at the planning stage to make sure everything has been considered.

Considerations for planning document production

Before you start your business document, it is important to know exactly what is required. Business documents are a reflection of the organisation and create an impression on the reader about your standards. When planning your document, it is important to consider the points shown in Table 3.5.

Table 3.5: Planning your document will make it more effective

Point to consider	Information needed
Purpose	• why the document is needed • whether the business document is required to convey information, persuade people or entertain people • how the document will be delivered to its audience (i.e. in a document format and/or presentation) • who will be working on the document or contributing to its completion
Content	• how much detail is required • the structure and layout of the document • whether the document needs text, tables, columns, charts, images, etc.
Audience needs	• level of language to be used (formal or informal) • whether the audience will understand the content • how many people will see the document • the format of the document • whether the information needs to be presented to people • whether documents need to be printed out • use of colour
Deadline	• when the document needs to be completed by (you should schedule this in your calendar) • whether the deadline is for a draft version or the final version

Link it up

Go to Unit 2 to find more information about professional behaviours, task preparation, managing your time and workloads.

Once you have this information, you can plan the steps you will need to take to research and source the content, plan and structure the layout of the document, input the content and finalise the document.

What are the pitfalls of failing to plan?

A key task at the planning stage is to work with supervisors and colleagues to discuss the requirements so the finished document meets the requirements of the customer and organisation.

Considerations when researching information

Administrators must consider the following as part of the Copyrights, Designs and Patents Act 1988.

Intellectual property

This helps to prevent people from stealing or copying names of products or brands, inventions, the design or look of a product, things that are written, made or produced. The five different types of intellectual property are:

- designs
- drawings
- text
- music
- video.

Copyright

This is one area of intellectual property. It protects people's work and stops others from copying it and using it without permission. One example is photographs or images which may be found when using search engines to source pictures to use in documents. Some images are free to use, but for others, you will need to request permission and you may need to pay a fee. More information can be found at www.ico.org.uk.

The copyright symbol identifies material that is protected by copyright

Validity of sources

When researching information, it is vital that you check the source. You must choose a source that is credible, reliable and factual. Do not consider blogs as a valid source of evidence as they may contain people's opinions, which will not necessarily be factually correct.

Practise

1. Why is it important that people respect the design rights of others?
2. How will you check that you are not infringing copyright law?

Knowledge and application of standard layouts and conventions

Organisations use standard layouts when producing each of their business documents to define the company's brand or identity, as well as for consistency purposes. An organisation might display these standard layouts in their letters, invoices, leaflets, stationery items such as notepads and envelopes, business cards, packaging, invitations and even in presentation slides. It is important that you follow the company's policy and procedures when preparing your documents.

Some documents are more formal than others. The layout, as well as the contents of the document, must reflect this in order to correctly communicate the intended message.

Brand consistency helps people to remember and recognise your organisation

Minutes of meetings can vary too. They can be an informal and brief note of the discussion and agreed action points or a more formal record of the meeting. Check how these have been laid out in the past to ensure you follow a similar convention.

Applying organisation standards and requirements

When preparing a document, it is important to consider the organisation's standards and requirements.

- **CORPORATE BRANDING** – how the organisation presents itself to the public (name, lettering, logo, strapline, colours etc.)
- **HOUSE STYLE** – the style of document presentation used by all staff in the organisation – document layout, type and size of font, size of margins, style of headings, position of the company logo, content of headers and footers etc.)
- **TONE OF VOICE** – the expressions and language used in the document to reflect the personality and values of the organisation
- **VERSION CONTROL** – a method of managing multiple variations of the same document so it is clear how the document has developed over time and which is the current version
- **APPROVAL PROCEDURES** – the process the organisation uses to check the final version of a document before allowing it to be sent to staff or customers.

> **Practise**
>
> 1 Choose two large organisations. Look at how they present themselves on their website or social media page. How many different logos do they have? Do these represent a different brand of the company?
>
> 2 Look at some utility bills at home. What do the branding and house style say about the organisation?

Using word-processing and presentation software

Once you have planned your document, researched information and gathered the content, the next stage is to prepare your document. Word-processing and presentation software are the two main software applications used to create business documents, depending on the content and purpose. If you are unfamiliar with these applications there are useful free and paid-for online tutorials to help. Your organisation may also offer training and support.

Word-processing software

Take a look at some of the leaflets and documents that come through your letterbox at home. What makes them interesting to look at? When designing business documents, administrators must consider the design, layout and structure.

Word-processing software is often used when creating common business documents. In most applications software, you can use one of the many templates available or you can design your own document. You will probably combine text with graphics, tables or images and collect information from other sources to make the document more interesting and attractive to your readers.

Presentation software

If you need to produce something more advanced and animated, you may need to consider using presentation software. This allows you to combine text and images with a range of other features. You may need to embed sound and video so start by choosing the most appropriate software application for your task. Planning the design of the document is important so the finished product is accurate, polished and professional.

Within each software application, you can choose to create a document from scratch or choose from one of the templates. Your organisation may require you to use a standard document or house style so check this before you start.

Word-processing and presentation software are both productivity software and they each have roles in creating specific document types. Word-processing software is predominantly text-based and presentation software is graphics-based.

Each type of software has a number of functions, as shown in Table 3.6.

Table 3.6: The functions of word-processing and presentation software

Word-processing software	Presentation software
Enter and edit text	Slide master – create the same slide throughout the presentation
Templates – choose from a range of templates or design your own (background, colours, font style, font size)	Templates – choose from a range of templates or design your own (background, colours, font style, font size)
Layout – change the margins, page orientation, paper size and columns	Layout – choose from a range of layouts depending on the content for each slide
Cut and paste – delete text or images, copy or move them to another place	Speaker notes – add comments or prompts for the speaker for each slide
Tables – create and format tables and graphs	Handouts – produce handouts for the audience (e.g. having three slides on a handout or each slide as a handout)
Find and replace – search for a specific word or phrase and change it (particularly useful in a long document)	Import content from other applications software into your slides, including audio and video files
Graphics – create your own or choose from existing shapes, smart art and types of chart	Graphics – create your own or choose from existing shapes, smart art and types of chart
Comments – highlight part of the text and add comments or suggestions for your reader	Header and footer – can be added to the slide and the handouts
Mail merge – create standard letters which can easily be personalised with names and addresses from a database	Animations – can be added to the content of a slide and transitions between slides
Grammar and spell-checking tools	Grammar and spell-checking tools

Think about what you are producing and the best way to present it

Practise

You have been asked by your manager to prepare for an event taking place next month.

1. Prepare a letter inviting clients to the event and asking them to confirm their attendance.
2. Prepare a poster that can be attached to the letter.
3. Produce a form that you can use to log attendance at the event.

B3 Checking fitness-for-purpose of business documents

Once your document is finished, it must be fit-for-purpose, clear and accurate. The content should comply with organisational requirements and legislation. Make sure you use all the tools and techniques of the software to check your document.

Considerations for checking content

Sending out documents without the correct checking procedures is not good practice. It is important that you check your work as you go along. Always make sure you check with the person requesting the document that you have full and accurate information about the content required and the format of the final document.

When you are preparing your document, check the accuracy and validity of the original information used. Check names, facts, statistics, dates and quotations. Cross-check any calculations you may have to do as part of a table, graph or chart you are producing.

If you are using graphics or photographs in your document, make sure you seek copyright approval for their use from the original source. Also check that you are complying with confidentiality issues and regulatory and organisational requirements.

Once you have finalised your document, it is important that it is reviewed before final sign-off. Some companies have official sign-off procedures and document control, particularly if they operate to national or international standards (for example, ISO 9001).

Link it up

Go to Unit 1 to find more information about your legal responsibilities.

Knowledge and use of tools and techniques for checking accuracy, format and layout

There are methods and software functions that can help you to check accuracy, format and layout as you go along and when you finish your document, as shown in Table 3.7.

Checking method	Details
Proofreading	Carefully reading through a document before it is printed to check for errors in spelling, grammar and punctuation.
Automated spelling and grammar check	Checking the accuracy of your work when using word-processing and presentation software. It will suggest corrections or identify repeated words. It is important you know how to check and alter the preferences in your software package to gain maximum benefit from this function.
Print preview	This automated function allows you to check on screen what your document will look like if printed out. You can check the margins, page breaks and images, and fix things before printing to avoid wasting time and paper.
Feedback from team members/peer review	Where appropriate, you can ask your team members to review your document to get their feedback before finalising the document.

Table 3.7: Methods and tools for checking accuracy

Below is a step-by-step guide for planning, checking and finalising a business document. The checklists below each step will help to ensure you consider each point listed at each stage before moving onto the next one, and to ensure the document is fit for business purposes.

STEP BY STEP — **BUSINESS DOCUMENTS**

STEP 1 Plan and design your document.

STEP 2 Check all the requirements have been met.

STEP 3 Check your document carefully.

STEP 4 Get your document approved, apply the correct document control details and save in the correct place.

Preparing document
- ☐ Planning
- ☐ Research
- ☐ Applications software
- ☐ Tools and techniques
- ☐ Design
- ☐ Validity of source information

Meeting requirements
- ☐ Fitness-for-purpose
- ☐ Copyright approval
- ☐ Feedback from others
- ☐ Compliance with organisational requirements and legislation
- ☐ Confidentiality

Final check
- ☐ Format and layout
- ☐ Proofreading
- ☐ Spelling and grammar check
- ☐ Print preview
- ☐ Peer review

Sign-off
- ☐ Appropriate person
- ☐ Document control
- ☐ Saving conventions

B4 Storing business documents following organisational requirements

When producing electronic documents and hard copies, it is important that you store them correctly so that you can easily find them again and to comply with legislation and your organisation's requirements.

Complying with organisational requirements

Saving your work by using appropriate names for files and folders is essential to maintain a professional image and to be able to find the document easily.

It is important to know where to store your documents and to carry out 'housekeeping' at regular intervals to delete files you no longer require or move them to a more suitable location. Figure 3.5 shows some important steps to remember when saving and storing your work.

UNIT 3 USING BUSINESS TECHNOLOGY TO PROCESS AND COMMUNICATE INFORMATION

SAVE
- Save your work as soon as you start a new document
- Create a new folder to store your file if you need to
- Save your work as you go along

NAME
- Use a name for your file/folder that is meaningful and descriptive
- Keep it short
- Be consistent
- Use letters and numbers. Avoid using special characters such as %, * or @ as some systems cannot read them
- Use dates in your filename, e.g. 120517
- Use version numbers e.g. V2.1
- Avoid spaces as some systems cannot read them. Use the underscore e.g. Greenwood_Project_Minutes_220417

EXTENSION
- Starts with a full stop after the filename e.g. .jpg, .docx, .pdf
- Lets the user know which application to use to open the file
- Consider the user (they may not have the latest version of application or have the software associated with the file)

LOCATION
- Save your work to your own directory
- Save to a shared directory if other people need access to your file
- Save to the Cloud if your organisation requires this
- You may need the email address of the other user(s). Always send passwords separately

Figure 3.5: If you fail to save your work and store it in the correct place you could cost the business time and create more work

There may be times when you don't want to send the original document to a customer. In these cases, you may send a PDF (portable document format) version of the document instead. This allows the customer to view the document on any computer but does not allow them to make changes (unless they have design editing software).

If a customer does not have the current version of the software, you can save a document in an earlier version. Remember that some of the features within the document may not be available or may work differently in earlier versions. To check how this may affect your document, you can turn on 'Compatibility Mode'.

> **Link it up**
>
> Go to Unit 1 to find more information about saving and storing business documents in line with your organisation's requirements.

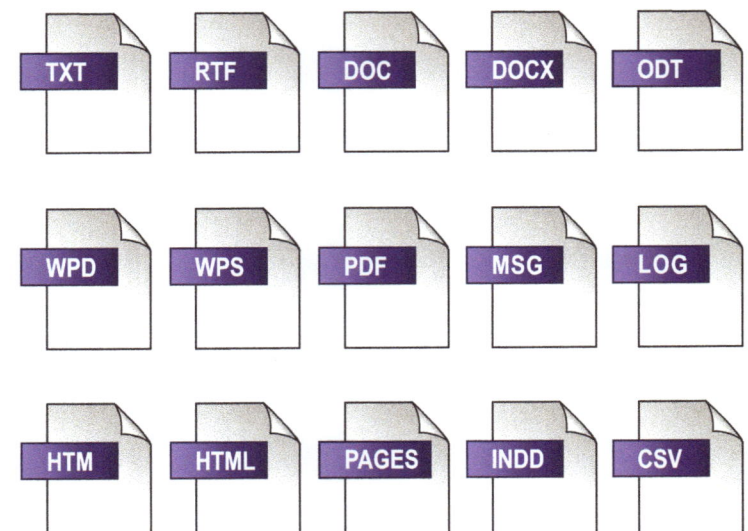

Many software applications allow you to save documents in different formats and versions, producing different file extensions

Methods of digital storage

When using a computer, you usually store files to a specific area that only you can access. However, where other team members need to access files, they can be stored in a shared network drive or the cloud.

Shared network drives

Do not store files that are confidential in a shared network drive. You can protect files by applying a password. If other people need access to a file that is password protected, make sure you provide the password separately and securely.

Business documents can be created, edited and stored using web-based applications such as Google Docs™. Files can be accessed by authorised personnel from any computer or device with an Internet connection.

Google Docs™ is a common web-based application for sharing documents

Cloud storage

Some companies use **THE CLOUD**, which is a form of digital storage using remote servers, usually managed by a hosting company. Examples of cloud-based storage include Dropbox™, Google Drive™, Apple iCloud® and SharePoint®.

The cloud allows you to access your documents anywhere on most devices (providing you have Internet access). It also allows you to work with other people in different locations. Some companies use cloud storage to back up their data on a daily or regular basis in case their own systems go down. Data security is important when using any cloud-based storage system and passwords can help reduce the risk of unauthorised access.

Methods of physical storage

Storing documents correctly in **HARD COPY** format, i.e. physically rather than digitally, is important so you (and authorised personnel) can find them easily. Whatever the size of your organisation, physical storage is essential where printed copies are required.

Although most documents are now stored electronically, filing cabinets are widely used as physical storage

Filing cabinets

Filing cabinets are an ideal place to store documents as they are lockable. This helps you to comply with data protection legislation and maintain confidentiality. Information can be stored alphabetically, numerically or chronologically (in date order). Be careful to store documents in the correct place; otherwise they may be difficult to retrieve.

Documents can also be filed in ring binders or lever arch folders. This allows similar documents or projects to be filed together and retrieved easily. The folders can easily be kept on your desk or a shelf, or stored away in a lockable cupboard if the information is sensitive or confidential.

Information resource facilities

In larger organisations, documents and other information may be stored in a central place such as an information resource facility. This may be similar to the learning resources centre or library at your school or training provider. You may need to allow extra time to file or access documents and there may be restricted areas due to the nature of the contents.

Skills and knowledge check

☐ I can give five examples of business documents.
☐ I can explain why we use business documents.
☐ I can describe three functions of word-processing software.
☐ I can describe three functions of presentation software.
☐ I can produce, check, save and share business documents.
☐ I can save my work correctly.

○ I know why it's important to use corporate branding and follow house style.
○ I know how to seek approval for my final documents.
○ I know how to apply version control to my documents.

C Use web-based technology to communicate and share information

C1 Using different types of web-based technology

The Internet has revolutionised the way that administrators work. It allows you to research, communicate and share information in a short space of time through the use of computers and networks.

Intranet

An intranet is a private network accessible only by an organisation's employees over the Internet. Login details are required to access the intranet to maintain security and confidentiality. As an administrator you will need to know its capabilities. The intranet can be used to:

- share information such as organisational policies and procedures
- store the current staff directory
- access bespoke software
- communicate and collaborate with colleagues.

Tasks that you could be asked to complete in your role as an administrator within the organisation's intranet might include:

- accessing and updating information saved on the intranet
- sending instant messages within the organisation
- uploading documents and videos to the intranet
- archiving outdated information that may need to be retrieved in the future.

It is important that you use the appropriate tools for each task.

Email software

An email is a message sent electronically to communicate with people internal or external to an organisation.

Uses

Emails are a quick way to communicate but they can be open to misinterpretation if they are not written clearly. Emails should not be used where discussion or interaction is required.

Emails can be sent to a single person or multiple people. If you regularly need to send email to a specific group of people (for example the sales team or those working on a specific project), it is worth setting up a 'group email' – choose an appropriate name for the group and add the email addresses of the people you want to include in the group, then save it to your address book. You will be able to add, remove or edit members of each group.

Selecting and using appropriate tools

Examples of email software include Microsoft Outlook®, Mac Mail® and Mozilla Thunderbird®. Each type of email software will have a different layout and different features but the tools to create an email and complete a range of tasks are the same.

Formatting messages

An email can be sent in one of three formats.
- HTML – this is the best format to use if you want to create messages with various fonts, colours, bullets and numbered points, or if you want to show pictures inside your message.
- Plain text – this format works for all email software but does not support (and will not display) bold or italic text, coloured fonts or other text formatting. Pictures cannot be sent inside the message but can be sent as attachments.
- Rich Text Format (RTF) – this format is supported only by Outlook® and some versions of Microsoft Exchange Client®.

Attaching files

When attaching a document, remember to consider the size of the file and any restrictions surrounding file access. Use the 'paper clip' icon to browse the folders on your computer and select the file or files you wish to send. If the file is too large to send, you may need to consider an alternative method of sending the file or reduce its size. You can select a number of files to be attached to an email and create a folder. You may be able to send small files without reducing their size. Alternatively, for larger files you can create a compressed (zipped) folder.

Figure 3.6 shows an example of an email that has been sent from one colleague to another, from within the same organisation. Table 3.8 explains each numbered section.

BTEC LEVEL 2 TECHNICAL CERTIFICATE BUSINESS ADMINISTRATION

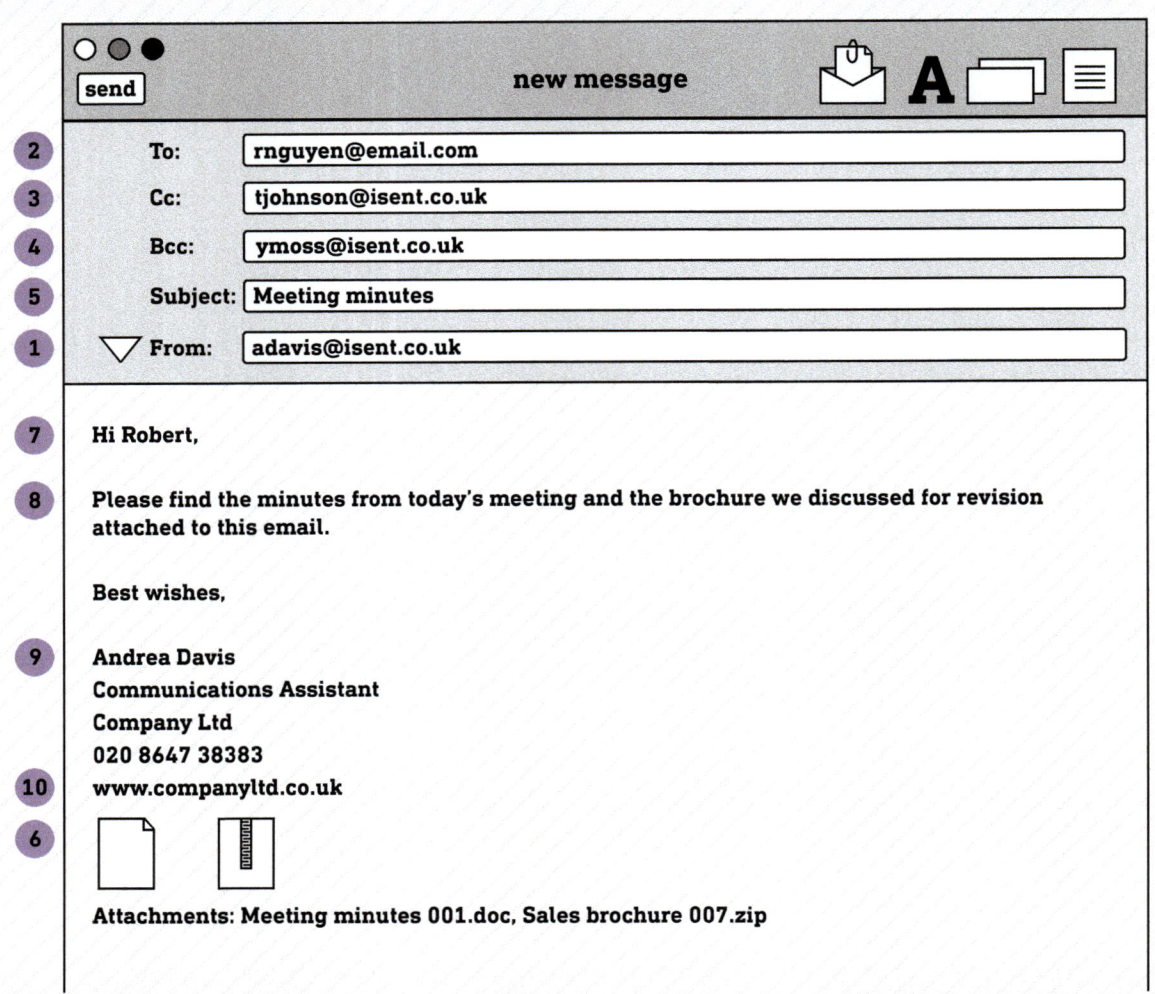

Figure 3.6: An example of an internal email

Table 3.8: The key features of an email

Feature	Email component	Description
1	From	The email address from which you wish to send the email.
2	To	This is the email of the person to whom you are sending the email (the recipient).
3	Cc	This stands for 'carbon copy'. This is used to let someone else know about the message you are sending. 'Cc' recipients are visible to all other recipients.
4	Bcc	This stands for 'blind carbon copy'. This is similar to 'carbon copy' but 'Bcc' recipients are not visible to anyone.
5	Subject	Lets the recipients know what the email is about.
6	Attachment	You can add files that are relevant to the email.
7	Salutation	Depending on how formal/informal the email is, you could start the email with 'Dear', 'Hello', or 'Hi' and add the person's name.
8	Body of the message	Should be short and to the point.
9	Signature	The end part of an email that tells the recipient who you are.
10	Hyperlink	Takes the recipient to another page on their web browser.

UNIT 3 | USING BUSINESS TECHNOLOGY TO PROCESS AND COMMUNICATE INFORMATION

Images and tables

If you are sending pictures by email, the best file formats are .jpg, .png and .gif. Avoid .tif and .bmp files. You may need to go into the original software and change the settings of an image before sending it by email.

Inserting hyperlinks

When composing your email, you may need to provide a hyperlink to take your recipients to another location in their web browser. To change text or an image to a hyperlink, select it, then on the 'Insert' tab, click on 'Hyperlink' to provide the relevant web details. Hyperlinks will usually appear in blue, underlined text and the mouse cursor will change to a pointing finger when you hover over a hyperlink. Hyperlinks can be inserted in both text and images.

Email signatures

An **EMAIL SIGNATURE** is the text used to finish your email. It will usually include your name, contact details and job description. They can also include a company logo and website address. When adding the email signature, close the message with 'Kind regards' or 'Best wishes' followed by your name, title and your organisation's contact details, particularly if you are sending an external email. Follow your organisation's house style as it can sometimes use specific fonts, colours and sizes. You can store and select different signatures in the email software, depending on your job roles and responsibilities.

Delivery receipts

'Delivery receipt' and 'Read receipt' are useful features of email software to confirm that a message you have sent has been delivered and read by the recipient.

Practise

You have been asked to respond to an email. A customer is trying to book tickets for an event that your company is hosting in three months' time. The customer states that the link on your website is not working.

Reply to the customer by email and include the following details.

- Thank the customer for their interest in the event.
- Apologise for the inconvenience.
- Provide the correct link to the company's event.
- Offer the customer a 10 per cent discount on their booking, using the code EVENT10.

Different forms of online collaboration software

Administrators may need to collaborate and communicate in real time with other colleagues and customers. Online collaboration software (e.g. Skype™ or WebEx™) can be used specifically to allow people to speak to and see each other at the same time in different locations using a computer, laptop, tablet or smartphone. Documents can also be shared with participants during video conferencing to allow people to edit and comment on them.

Shared drive workspace

Another way for authorised people to access shared files is by using a shared drive workspace (e.g. SharePoint®, Google Docs™ or Dropbox™). This may be accessed via the intranet or via a cloud-based service and enables authorised users to work on documents in real time.

> **Practise**
>
> 1 Research the three different types of online collaboration software listed above that support video conferencing. Describe the capabilities of each one.
>
> 2 Research the three different shared drive workspaces listed above. Explain the benefits and limitations of each one.

Instant messaging

Instant messaging (e.g. Google Hangouts™) is a type of chat that offers real-time text messaging using the Internet. Advanced features also enable the use of hyperlinks, audio and file transfer.

Online collaboration software can also be used without video and allows users to share slide presentations and documents in real time. Users cannot see one another but can request to speak to the group by notifying the presentation organiser. Instant messaging or (text chat) is also available for users to send a message to an individual or the group. This type of software may be useful for training purposes across a large organisation.

Video conferencing

Examples of video conferencing include:

- Skype™ – useful for individual or group meetings where the delegates can see one another; allows instant messaging
- WebEx™ – useful for online meetings or webinars, screen sharing and demonstrations of products/services
- Google Hangouts™ – useful for online meetings, live broadcasts, screen sharing and instant messaging.

What should you do to prepare for video conference calls to ensure everything runs smoothly?

It is important to prepare for video conference calls so everything runs smoothly on the day. You will need to be organised and so will your presenter and delegates. Provide them with correct login details ahead of the scheduled event, as well as agenda items and details of any documents they will need to have available at the time of the video conference. You may need to assist during the video conference call by checking instant messages so nothing is missed and allowing screen sharing to relevant documents. You may also need to liaise with technicians in case there are any technical issues during the conference call.

> **Practise**
>
> Your manager has asked you to set up a video conference with six other delegates to be held in two weeks' time. Four of the delegates work from home and two will need to attend their local hub.
>
> 1 Make a list of your preparations for the video conference in the order that you need to do each task.
>
> 2 Why is it important that you and your delegates prepare for the video conference in advance?

Social media

Social networking is a way of communicating with people to share information, photographs and videos over the Internet. This can be for personal use but organisations are increasingly using social media for business use, specifically to:

- communicate with existing and new customers
- promote new products
- inform customers of services and offers
- provide customer reviews.

Social media is interactive and allows organisations to have an online presence. Customers and colleagues can comment and engage in conversations relating to the organisation's posts, news or events. If you are responsible for replying to comments posted on social media, it is important to follow your organisation's policies and protocol.

Increasingly, organisations are using social media like those in Table 3.9 (continued on next page) to communicate with customers.

> **Link it up**
>
> Go to Unit 2 to find more information about professional behaviours and meeting organisational expectations.

Table 3.9: Examples of social networking for business

Facebook®	
Key features	- Private messaging - Video/photo news feeds - Posts/notifications - Carrying out polls - Encouraging feedback from followers/customers
Main uses	- Create an audience and grow relationships with followers - Provide updates - Promote an event - Increase website traffic - Market products/services and promotional videos and photos - Live-stream events

Table 3.9: Examples of social networking for business

Twitter®		
Key features	• Hashtag options • Allows tweets of 140 characters • Posts/notifications • Direct messages	
Main uses	• Share quick pieces of information • Grow networks/customer bases • Promote an event • Market products/services and promotional videos and photos	
Instagram®		
Key features	• Photos/video posts • Share stories – last 24 hours • Hashtag options • Direct messages • Posts/comments • Live video streaming	
Main uses	• Post images and short videos without the sales pitch • Launch new products and services • Promote examples of work • Promote services and exclusive deals	
LinkedIn®		
Key features	• Private messages • Business profiles/CVs • Make professional connections	
Main uses	• Advertise jobs • Connect with other professionals • Participate in group discussions • Promote new products/services	

Practise

Your organisation is holding an event to launch a new product. How will you use social media to promote the event? Write a plan outlining specific activities you will do:

1. a month before the event
2. the week before the event
3. the day before the event
4. on the day of the event.

Using web-based technology can result in measurable benefits for organisations by providing:

- more organisational effectiveness and efficiency
- secure and consistent access to information
- improved communications.

These can ultimately result in reduced business costs so it is important that an administrator is able to use them appropriately.

C2 Creating, communicating and sharing business information using web-based technology

When planning your web-based communications, it is important to know exactly what is required. Web-based communications reflect the organisation and create an impression about your standards.

Considerations in planning web-based communications

In order to plan a web-based event, you need to consider the points listed in Table 3.10.

Table 3.10: Planning a web-basec event

Points to consider	Details
Audience needs	<ul><li>How many people will see the content?</li><li>What level of language should be used (formal or informal)?</li><li>How accessible is the information?</li><li>What depth of information is needed?</li></ul>
Communication medium	<ul><li>Is the communication internal or external to the organisation?</li><li>How long is the communication?</li><li>Will it be received by individuals or groups of people?</li><li>Will communication be in person or in writing?</li><li>What depth of information is needed?</li></ul>
Timeliness	<ul><li>Prepare a plan to meet the necessary deadlines.</li><li>Prepare a plan of activities for using web-based communications.</li><li>Have a **CONTINGENCY** plan.</li></ul>
Confidentiality	<ul><li>Commercially sensitive material should not be in the public domain.</li><li>Do not share confidential material with unauthorised people.</li></ul>
Accuracy and validity of information	<ul><li>Proofread your work.</li><li>Check your work as you go along.</li><li>Use credible and reliable sources.</li><li>Acknowledge reference sources.</li><li>Check the content is sound.</li><li>Check your spelling, punctuation and grammar.</li></ul>
Compliance with policy and procedures	<ul><li>Check that you are **COMPLIANT** with your organisation's policies and procedures relating to security, social media, encryption, data protection, use of passwords, use of logos and house style.</li></ul>

Use of acceptable language and tone

It is important to remember that any business communication requires language and tone that is appropriate to the content and its audience. Some communications may need to be more formal than others and administrators should ensure the language and tone are fit-for-purpose.

Different types of audience

When communicating information, consider your audience. Is your target audience colleagues, managers, existing or potential customers or the general public?

Once you know your target audience, you can prepare your communication to suit their needs. It will help you to select the appropriate language and tone for your content.

Considerations for sharing information

When sharing information, it is important to remember to share the content with authorised people only. You should not share confidential or commercially sensitive material with the general public as this can go viral in a short space of time and be used by competitors. You must also consider where you will store your files and how the files will be named.

Impact and consequences for the organisation

Failure to follow legislation, regulations and your organisation's policies and procedures could result in some serious consequences for your company. Information can travel quickly when using web-based technology so even if you remove a link or take a post down on social media, the information will be in the public domain.

Once information is made public, the impact can be catastrophic. Examples of such consequences are:

- a risk to the organisation's reputation
- losing custom from existing or potential customers
- negative publicity going viral (being widely shared on social media)
- criminal or legal action being taken.

As an administrator, it is important to ask if you are not sure about something at any stage of the planning and design process. Never communicate and share information over the Internet if you have any doubts about what you are sharing.

> **Link it up**
>
> Go to section B4, 'Storing business documents following organisational requirements', to find out more about using appropriate file-naming conventions and selecting storage locations.

Skills and knowledge check

- [ ] I can list three examples of online collaboration software.
- [ ] I can describe three benefits of using web-based technology.
- [ ] I can use appropriate language and tone when producing written communications.
- [ ] I have practised using different types of web-based technology.

- ○ I know what is meant by web-based technology.
- ○ I know why it's important to maintain security and confidentiality when using the Internet.

Ready for assessment

You will need to show that you can use business technology to process and communicate information. You need to provide evidence that you have:

- used computer equipment to enter, edit and organise information
- used data management software (databases and spreadsheets)
- extracted, analysed and manipulated business information for specific reporting needs
- used word-processing software
- used presentation software
- designed and produced at least two accurate business documents, meeting quality standards
- applied more advanced software tools and techniques when using standard or bespoke software
- complied with procedures relating to information security and confidentiality
- complied with legal requirements and organisational procedures
- used web-based technology
- complied with acceptable behaviours when using web-based technology.

Evidence could take the form of:

- a reflective account
- screen shots
- document printouts
- observation records.

Witness testimonies can also be used to confirm the work that you have done. Don't forget that any work-based evidence needs to be counter-signed by your workplace supervisor and dated.

In order to improve your performance at work, it is useful for you to reflect on what you have done so far. Outline three ways in which you have learned from your experiences and explain how you will apply this learning to improve your performance in the future.

BTEC LEVEL 2 TECHNICAL CERTIFICATE BUSINESS ADMINISTRATION

WORK FOCUS

HANDS ON

There are some important occupational skills and competencies that you will need to practise which relate to this unit. Below are some actions that you should carry out and some that you shouldn't, as you develop your skills further.

Skills	Do	Don't
Using computing equipment	• Follow procedures and read manufacturer's instructions carefully • Be aware of health and safety procedures • Store your portable devices securely when not in use	• Give out your password • Forget to take a break from using your screen • Try to repair electrical equipment yourself • Forget to keep your equipment clean
Researching information	• Confirm specific requirements • Check the validity of source data	• Forget to check if approval is required for images, information and documents • Forget to keep source data
Using spreadsheets and databases	• Check the accuracy of source data • Check the accuracy of your content • Use the correct formulae • Use the correct reporting queries • Use the most appropriate chart or graph to display your spreadsheet information	• Forget to check the validity of your data
Producing business documents	• Choose the software to suit the requirements • Follow the house style for the format and layout of your document • Check your work carefully • Ask for feedback on your documents	• Forget to plan your document first • Forget to allow time for revisions to your document • Leave confidential documents on your desk • Forget to save your work regularly
Storing files	• Choose a meaningful filename • Use the correct file extension • Password protect confidential files • Give access to authorised users of shared files • Check the storage space available on your computer or device	• Keep personal data for longer than needed • Forget to delete files that are no longer needed
Using emails	• Check you are sending the email to the correct recipient(s) • Include a subject that is meaningful • Communicate the information clearly • Compress files if you are sending large attachments • Use folders to organise your work	• Send lengthy emails – attach a separate document if necessary • Send emails without checking them first • Forget your signature • Forget to clean out your inbox and delete emails that are no longer needed
Using online collaboration software	• Give your recipients notice of an online meeting or video conference • Prepare information and documents in advance of online events • Check equipment will work prior to online events • Allow enough preparation time	• Store confidential files in a shared workspace

UNIT 3 | USING BUSINESS TECHNOLOGY TO PROCESS AND COMMUNICATE INFORMATION

Using social media	• Follow protocol when posting and replying to comments • Use images and text • Use the features of the social media platform to the maximum • Check your content is accurate	• Share confidential or commercially sensitive information • Post personal opinions
Working as part of a team	• Discuss ideas for a new project or presentation • Help to turn ideas into practical solutions	• Ignore online business technology when collaborating with others
Respecting colleagues and others who you work with	• Consider the needs of others • Only share information with those who need access	• Forget to maintain security and confidentiality
Using appropriate communication with colleagues and customers	• Use the correct tone of voice	• Use jargon or over-complicated language

Ready for work?

Take this short quiz to find out whether you'd be the person chosen for that dream job.

1 You need to work in another office without a fixed Internet connection. You should take a:
- [ ] A laptop
- [ ] B tablet or smartphone
- [ ] C desktop computer
- [ ] D pen and paper.

2 To check the validity of your source data you should:
- [ ] A ask your manager
- [ ] B use data validation tools
- [ ] C ask your colleague
- [ ] D check copyright.

3 You need to present some figures. You should prepare:
- [ ] A a leaflet
- [ ] B a spreadsheet or graph
- [ ] C an email
- [ ] D a letter.

4 You are working on a new project. Your colleagues work all over the country. The best way to discuss progress and screen share is to use:
- [ ] A Google Hangouts™
- [ ] B Skype™
- [ ] C telephone
- [ ] D email.

5 Your colleague is carrying out a risk assessment of your workstation. This is a requirement under the:
- [ ] A Data Protection Act
- [ ] B Display Screen Equipment Regulations
- [ ] C Computer Misuse Act
- [ ] D Equality Act.

Your score:

Answers: 1A, 2B, 3B, 4A, 5B

If you scored full marks, you are ready for a role in using business technology to process and communicate information. If you got two or more answers wrong, you may need to brush up on your business technology skills.

127

4 Planning, Organising and Supporting Business Events

Could you communicate effectively with key people in an organisation? Most organisations communicate directly and indirectly through events such as team meetings, conferences or exhibitions. Providing effective and efficient administrative support before, during and after business events is vital to their success.

In this unit, you will develop key knowledge and skills from previous units and learn how to plan, organise and support business events by producing an event plan, taking minutes and sourcing event resources including venues. You will learn to support participants during events and ensure that queries and complaints are resolved, by using appropriate verbal and non-verbal communication skills.

How will I be assessed?

You will need to work within a business setting, undertaking focused activities which provide opportunities to plan, organise and support a business event. You will be given an event brief and you will create and follow an event plan to prepare for the event. You will perform various tasks, including sourcing information about venues and working with others to organise equipment and resources.

You will be observed providing support during the event, which may include taking minutes, responding to queries or problems and gathering feedback. You will carry out follow-up activities such as finalising minutes ready for distribution and analysing event feedback.

You will produce evidence to show that you have successfully planned, organised and supported the event. This may include signed witness testimonies or observation sheets, an event plan, an event brief, venue searches, event materials, minutes and feedback forms.

Assessment criteria

Pass	Merit	Distinction
Learning aim A: Plan and prepare for a business event according to a given brief		
A.P1 Produce a basic plan for a business event that meets the requirements of the given brief.	**A.M1** Produce a detailed plan for a business event and make comprehensive preparations that align with the plan and brief and include actions taken to mitigate potential problems.	**AB.D1** Evaluate the effectiveness of the planning, preparations and support activities for the event.
A.P2 Make satisfactory preparations for a business event that aligns with the event plan and the given brief.		
Learning aim B: Provide administrative support to a business event in accordance with business needs		
B.P3 Provide adequate support during a business event, handling tasks and queries satisfactorily and demonstrating professional and helpful behaviours.	**B.M2** Provide dedicated support during a business event, demonstrating technical ability and professionalism in handling tasks and resolving queries and issues.	
Learning aim C: Carry out follow-up activities after a business event		
C.P4 Carry out post-event follow-up activities in line with the event plan and brief, including gathering feedback from participants.	**C.M3** Evaluate the feedback from participants, using the appropriate business technology to analyse and present the results in an appropriate format.	**C.D2** Make justified recommendations for improving future events.

A Plan and prepare for a business event according to a given brief

A1 Agreeing an event brief

To ensure a business event runs smoothly and achieves its objectives, it is important to agree the event brief in advance. This information is likely to be provided by a colleague or manager; however, there may be occasions when you are the person responsible for setting a brief for a meeting or larger business event.

Different types of events

An event is a planned occasion where groups of people gather for the purpose of receiving or communicating information. Many different types of event may take place within an organisation including:

- **formal** – for example, meetings which require MINUTES to be produced or attendees to vote for actions to be carried out, to meet legal or regulatory requirements
- **informal** – for example, meetings or events which don't require any formal recording or legal obligations, such as team briefings
- **internal** – events which are attended by employees of the organisation and generally take place at the organisation's premises
- **external** – events which are attended by STAKEHOLDERS outside the organisation such as customers or suppliers.

Practise

Link the different events with the correct event types in Figure 4.1. Each event may link with more than one event type.

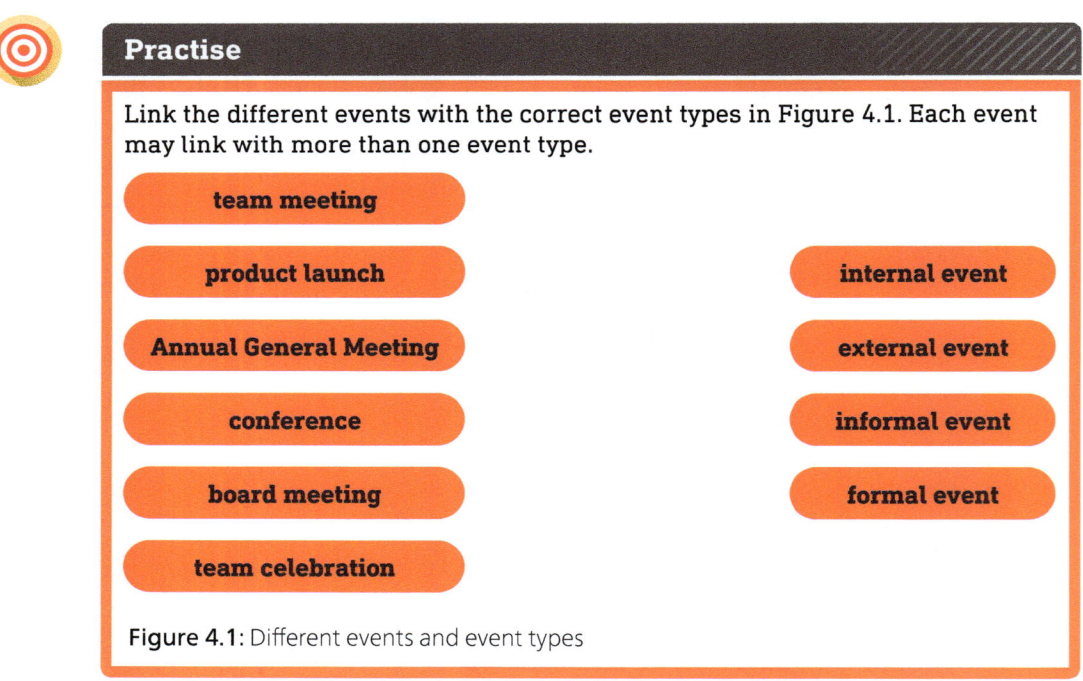

Figure 4.1: Different events and event types

The event brief

An event brief is used to confirm the purpose of the event and specify the event objectives. The event brief differs from the event plan.

- The *brief* is the **why, what, when, who** and **where** of the event.
- The *plan* is **how** the event will happen.

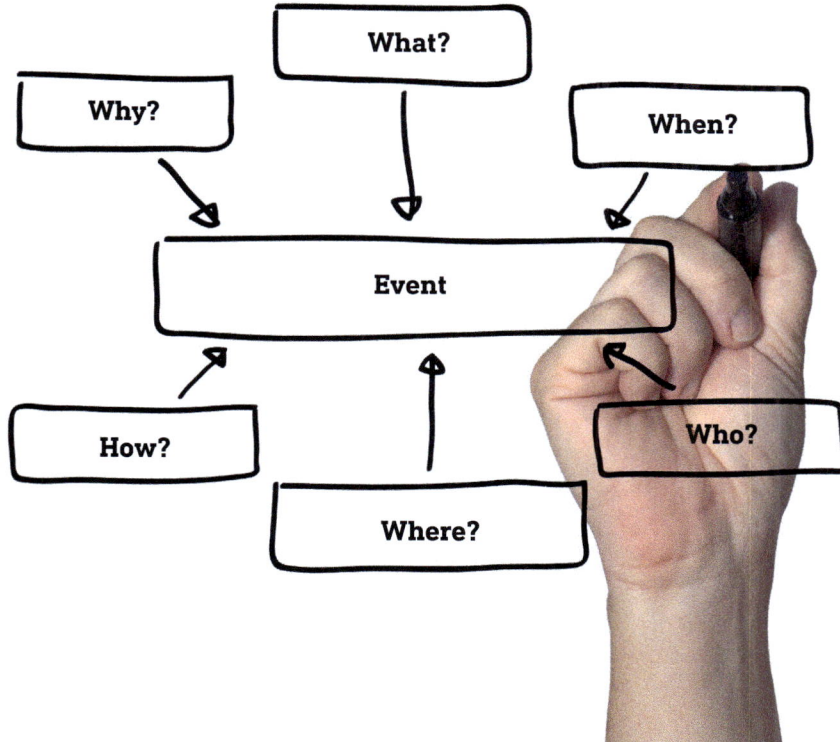

Brainstorming ideas will help you plan events

Information about the event may be provided verbally, for example within a meeting or a discussion, or as a written business **COMMUNICATION** such as an email or physical document. Regardless of how it is communicated, a standard event brief must include certain essential information, as shown in Figure 4.2.

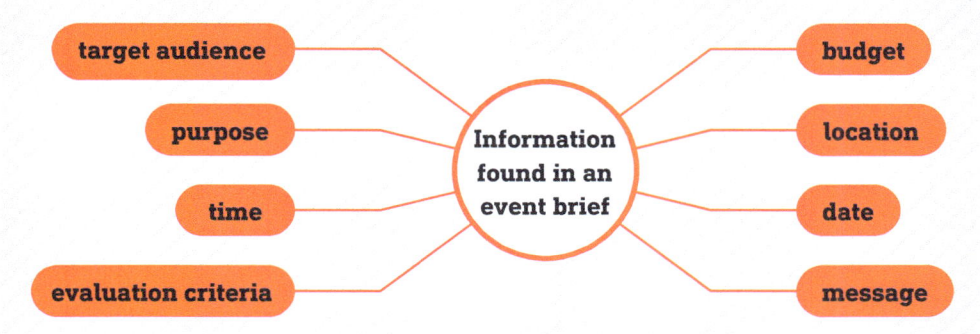

Figure 4.2: The basic requirements of an event brief

- **Purpose** – it is important to understand the purpose of the event to ensure the planning and preparations are relevant to that purpose and are likely to achieve the correct outcome.
- **Message** – the information to be communicated during the event.
- **Budget** – how much the organisation is prepared to spend on the event. Costs may include: hiring a venue, providing refreshments, booking travel and accommodation and the cost of producing resources. Budget is not a consideration for every internal event, e.g. staff meetings.
- **Date** – an agreed date which allows for the highest attendance. For more formal events such as disciplinary hearings or Annual General Meetings (AGM), the date of the event must support relevant legal requirements, particularly the amount of notice which needs to be provided to attendees.
- **Time** – events generally take place within an organisation's operating hours, for example between 9 a.m. and 5 p.m. However, some events may be held during the evening or on the weekend, such as an awards evening or a trade show. Time would also include the duration of the event.
- **Target audience** – who must attend or who the organisation would like to attend.
- **Location** – where the event is to be held, for example at the organisation's premises, a hired venue or a specific location such as a conference/exhibition centre.
- **Evaluation criteria** – these are based on the scope of the event plan and are the success criteria you will use to measure the effectiveness of the event, for example number of attendees, percentage of passes at a training event or number of sales leads generated.

The importance of agreeing a brief for an event

Have you ever been to an event that has been poorly organised? How did this impact on your impression of the event itself, the people delivering the event and, if applicable, the organisation hosting the event?

See Figure 4.3 for examples of negative event feedback.

Figure 4.3: Negative comments after an event

Comments of this nature are bad news for individuals, teams and organisations. They suggest that the person or team responsible for planning, preparing and organising the event has not understood the event brief or what the organisation needed to achieve from the event. Alternatively, the people who organised the event may not have had the foresight to predict issues which could arise during the event and deal with them efficiently and effectively.

The impact of poorly planned events could include:

- participants not receiving full or **ACCURATE** information
    - participants will not fully understand the topic being presented
    - key points or instructions will be missed
    - participants will become bored and disengaged from the event
    - incorrect information will be acted on
- participants being unlikely to attend similar events in the future
    - fewer opportunities to keep knowledge up to date
    - events not being cost effective to run
- risk to the organisation's reputation
    - loss of competitive advantage
    - existing or potential customers may take their business elsewhere
    - reputation for staging poor events
- financial losses
    - charges for venue, food and beverage services
    - event management fees and expenses
    - cost of booked accommodation
    - operational losses as a result of taking staff away from their daily work to attend events.

The failure of events is usually due to poor planning, organisation and support. It is true what they say: 'By failing to prepare, you are preparing to fail.'

Practise

Think about an event you have recently attended at work or at college. This could be a team meeting or college sport event you have been to.

1. Try creating an event brief based on what you know about the event you attended. Provide as much information as you can, referring to Figure 4.2 to see what you need to include.
2. Identify what was organised well and what wasn't so well organised about the event.
3. What improvements could be made so that a similar event would be more successful next time?

A2 Planning for an event

Once the brief for the event has been agreed and understood, the next stage is to use this information to plan the activities required to make the event happen. Event planning may involve multiple people or teams within the organisation, and external events management companies may be contracted to organise larger, more specialist events.

Roles and responsibilities

Where a team is responsible for organising an event, each member of the events team must understand their role and responsibilities before, during and after the event. If an organisation regularly holds events, it may employ dedicated events staff with specific responsibilities. In a company where events are organised as and when required, staff will take on events responsibilities and step into an events role when necessary.

The nature of the event will determine the specific team requirements, but most events teams will have a number of key roles, as shown in Table 4.1.

Table 4.1: Roles and responsibilities in event planning

Role	Responsibilities and duties
Event leader or event manager	Responsible for overseeing the event, making important decisions and signing off event briefs and plans. This person will ultimately be accountable for the success or failure of the event.
Event co-ordinator	Responsible for co-ordinating people and resources to ensure the event runs smoothly. This person will have strong leadership skills and will plan and allocate work activities to relevant support staff. They will regularly monitor the progress of agreed individual and team objectives to ensure the event plan stays on track.
Support staff	Responsible for supporting planning, preparation and delivery activities for the event. It is important that support staff maintain communication with their event co-ordinator and raise any issues or potential issues early in the event planning process.

Practise

Investigate a large-scale event such as the Ideal Home Exhibition or events held at large venues such as Olympia, or ExCel in London or the NEC in Birmingham.

What event management teams, roles and responsibilities do these organisations use when planning and organising large events?

Creating an event plan

Event plans can take many forms depending on the organisation, the team and the nature of the event. In most cases, a written record of the plan will be produced to enable effective communication, sharing of event information, monitoring of progress and amendment where required.

Formats of events plans, as shown in Figure 4.4, may include:
- **paper** – for example a printed action plan or Gantt chart
- **whiteboard** – good visibility within the workplace and easily updated during team briefings
- **electronic task management tools** – allow for individual tasks to be communicated and prioritised within work diaries
- **web-based collaborative software tools** – for example Microsoft® SharePoint or Microsoft® OneNote.

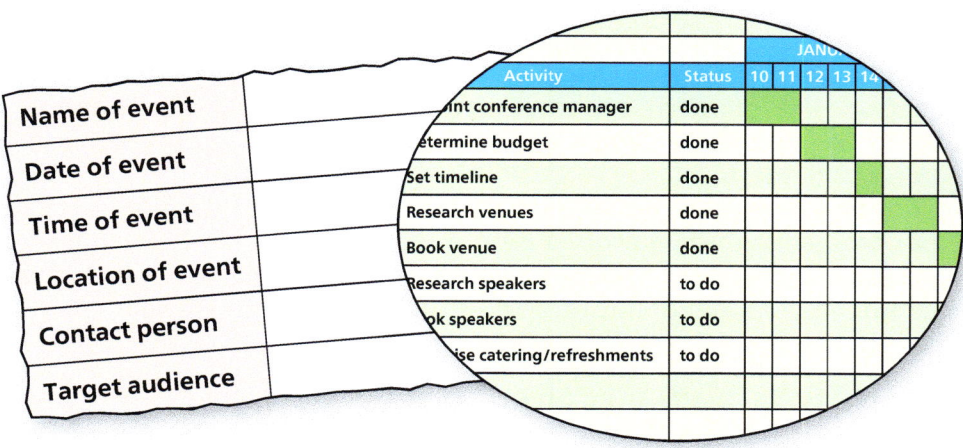

Figure 4.4: Examples of different event plan formats

Event plan principles

The key five elements of an effective event plan are shown in Figure 4.5.

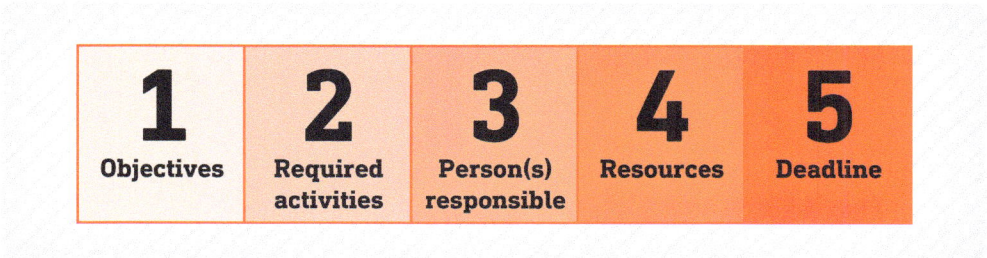

Figure 4.5: Five key principles of event planning

In addition to these five principles, an event plan also factors in a plan for when or if things go wrong.

- **Objectives** – what is the expected outcome of the event and how will this be achieved?
- **Required activities** – the specific actions which need to be taken in order to achieve the objectives. In an event plan, activities should begin with an active verb, for example prepare attendee invitations.
- **Person(s) responsible** – the person or people responsible for completing the required activity. This is usually decided by group agreement, a person volunteering to complete the activity or a person being nominated based on their skill set and ability to complete the task well.
- **Resources** – any relevant materials, equipment, people or information needed to complete the activity, for example a **LAMINATOR** to produce name badges or branded stationery to give to attendees. Resources may also include those needed for the event itself, such as audiovisual equipment.
- **Deadline** – the date and/or time that the activity needs to be completed by. The deadline must be realistic, based on the nature of the activity; therefore it is important to ask the person responsible how long the activity may take to complete. Always try to factor in spare time as a **CONTINGENCY**, just in case there are any setbacks.

- **Potential for risk and problems** – foreseeing any problems which may occur relating to people, equipment and resources, or time. Risks may include health, safety or security or going over budget. Problems may include lack of internet connection or equipment failure. Considering risks and problems in advance will allow you to plan contingencies to deal with these.
- **Contingency planning** – agreeing actions to be taken to address risks or problems which may occur before, during or after an event. It is essential to plan for the unexpected. Contingency plans may include an additional budget or having back-up equipment and information.

Considerations in planning an event

It is important to become skilled in recognising factors of an event which may not be obvious within an event brief. Some considerations are shown in Figure 4.6.

Individual needs and special requirements	Health, safety and security
• Physical disability • Hearing impediment • Visual impairment • Learning difficulty • Dietary requirements	• Maximum room capacity • Emergency procedures • Fire alarm testing • Risk and hazards • Welfare facilities • Secure cloakroom facilities • Access permissions and ID
Legal and organisational requirements	**Resources and materials**
• Health and safety • Food safety • Data protection • Confidentiality • Copyright and intellectual property • **POLICIES** and **PROCEDURES** • Code of conduct and behaviours • Brand promotion and reputation	• Spare equipment as a back-up • Presentation information in alternative formats • Spare participant packs • Stationery • Refreshments including licensing to sell alcohol

Figure 4.6: Event considerations

Event contracts

Organisations generally create a contract between themselves and the venue or event suppliers, to ensure all parties fulfil their responsibilities agreed within that contract. Valid contracts typically contain the following contractual points.

- **Parties of the contract** – this includes the organisation and suppliers, including the venue.
- **Contract date** – the date on which the services will be delivered.
- **Definitions used in the contract** – key words used in the contract.
- **Goods and services being provided or received** – including venue, catering or presenter fees.
- **Payment amount and payment date** – how much will services cost and when do suppliers require payment for providing their services?

UNIT 4 | PLANNING, ORGANISING AND SUPPORTING BUSINESS EVENTS

What if...?

You are an event organiser and have been made aware that one of the participants attending the event has a physical disability and uses a wheelchair.

1 Identify two factors that need to be considered when planning a venue for this event to ensure the participant can access all service areas and facilities.

2 Explain why it is necessary to meet the participant's individual needs.

Importance of agreeing an event plan

The event plan will be used to steer the event preparations and guide event staff to fulfil their allocated responsibilities, so this plan must be checked and agreed before preparations go ahead.

These checks will ensure that the plan is fit for purpose and will meet agreed business objectives, so the event will be a success.

The event manager or co-ordinator will be responsible for agreeing the event plan. Be prepared for feedback about changes which need to be made to the plan – this is normal and should be anticipated.

It is always beneficial to have another pair of eyes looking at planning documents because it can be very easy to overlook important factors. In addition, it would be helpful to have someone else's opinion, as they may be able to suggest more efficient and effective methods of doing things that weren't originally considered.

Link it up

Go to Unit 1 to find more information about the Equality Act 2010.

Link it up

Go to Unit 2 to find more information about planning and prioritising time and work activities as well as different tools and techniques for doing so.

A3 Making preparations for an event in line with agreed brief

How well you prepare for an event is the difference between success and failure. In this section, you will explore the different aspects of an event which require preparation activities.

How to source a venue, accommodation and travel

If you have ever booked a holiday or searched for a venue to host an event such as a celebration, or helped someone else with this kind of booking, you will have developed valuable knowledge and skills which will help you here. The principles for booking leisure and business venues are fundamentally the same – they just have different requirements and considerations.

What are the important aspects of a venue that you need to consider before making the booking?

Suitability for the type of event

The venue needs to be big enough to cater for large groups of people and specific event requirements.

Location

If the venue is to be held externally, should this be a city centre location or a tranquil countryside retreat? Accessibility for the target audience is a key consideration.

Facilities

The venue should meet the needs of the participants including parking, accommodation, restaurant or buffet services, leisure facilities and entertainment. Event organisers may require break out rooms or printed and prepared event materials.

Accessibility

How long it would take participants to get to the venue is a deciding factor as the organisation may have to pay to get staff to the location. Transport options such as car parking, nearby bus stops or train stations need to be considered, as well as accessibility within or around the building.

Technological capabilities

Technology and accessibility to the internet are essential requirements at most meetings. Considerations should include audiovisual technology, laptops, projector and screen, whiteboards, **VIDEO CONFERENCING** facilities and Wi-Fi connectivity.

Budget

Venues typically charge different rates for different sized rooms, depending on how many people a room will hold.

UNIT 4 | PLANNING, ORGANISING AND SUPPORTING BUSINESS EVENTS

> **What if...?**
>
> New technology has increased opportunities for businesses to explore more innovative, efficient and cost-effective ways to run events.
>
> What non-traditional methods and capabilities can be used when hosting/running an event (for example online booking for delegates attending a conference)?

Selecting a venue

The venue will be very much determined by the purpose of the event, event activities and the number of participants, as shown in Table 4.2.

Table 4.2: Event types and suitable venues

Event type	Venue
One-to-one meeting	Held within the organisation and requires seating for two people. Rooms must be suitable for discussions containing personal information.
Team meeting	Similar to a one-to-one meeting. This space must be sufficient in size to accommodate a larger group of people.
Board meeting and AGM	Due to the level of formality associated with board meetings and AGMs, organisations typically have a boardroom designed to accommodate all board members. A community-based organisation, such as a local football club, will have a venue to accommodate members of that organisation and wider audiences such as local residents.
Training session	Both internal and external venues may be used to host training sessions depending on the nature of the training being delivered. For 'off the job' training, a training room or suitable external venue may be used. 'On the job' training is likely to take place in the working environment. Also consider equipment for relevant activities.
Staff meeting and conference	Staff meetings may be held locally, regionally, nationally or internationally. It is unlikely that larger organisations will have capacity within their premises to host meetings or conferences of this size. Therefore an external venue will be required, for example, a hotel with large function rooms or a designated conferencing centre.
Tradeshow	Typically, tradeshow stands are agreed between the organisation, event promoters and venue in advance of the event. Pitch fees are determined by size.
Online events	A suitable location is required to host the event. This venue needs facilities to run ICT and audiovisual equipment as well as other business technology required to run virtual events such as a green screen studio.

Booking the venue, accommodation and travel

Most organisations have documented systems and procedures for booking external services. As an administrator, you need to be familiar with your organisation's service **procurement** processes (the act of obtaining or buying goods and services).

Booking procedures, as shown in Figure 4.7, may differ depending on the size of the room, the facilities required or the type of travel and accommodation required. Most hotels have online booking, which makes it easier for event organisers to book accommodation.

139

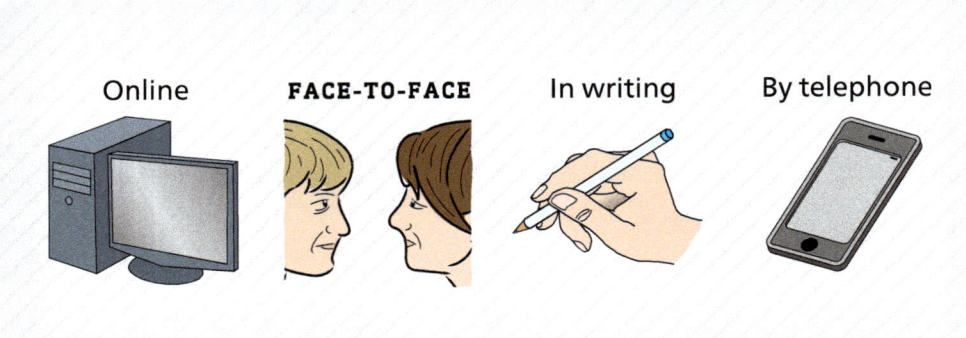

Figure 4.7: Different booking procedures

Organisations often have a documented 'Business Travel Policy' which contains information about restrictions and allowable expenses, and considerations when booking travel and accommodation for business purposes. Examples are shown in Table 4.3.

Table 4.3: Considerations when booking travel and accommodation

Travel	Accommodation
Select the most cost-effective mode of transport	Restricted budgets based on role within the organisation
Select the lowest logical fare	Accommodation costs include breakfast
Travel standard/economy class – not first or business class	Maximum spend on lunch and evening meals
Consider alternatives to travel, e.g. virtual events	Allowable expenses exclude alcoholic drinks
	Quality of accommodation based on number of stars and online customer reviews

Travel and accommodation should always meet the needs of travellers. It is important to consider individual requirements/situations including physical disabilities, whether they have a driving licence and access to a roadworthy vehicle, and distance to be travelled.

Booking terms and conditions

How you proceed with the booking will depend on the agreed payment terms and conditions, method of payment, whether a deposit or full payment is required in advance, invoicing procedures (including purchase orders) and how far in advance the event is. You should also be aware that some venues have a cancellation policy to cover their costs in the event of short notice cancellations.

Always get booking details checked before you confirm.

Ask your event co-ordinator or manager to check the booking details before you confirm. Failure to do this may result in the venue being too small or booked for the wrong date, which may be difficult and costly to rectify afterwards. A confirmed booking is a contract between your organisation and the venue and may be **LEGALLY BINDING**, which means that an agreement has been consciously made, and certain actions are now required.

Organising appropriate equipment and resources

Some venues will provide a full event management service. In this case all you need to do is specify equipment and resource requirements and provide relevant information to participants. In most cases, the administrator is responsible for organising equipment and resources.

Common items of equipment and resources required for meetings and events include the following.

- **Laptop** – operates appropriate presentation **SOFTWARE** required to deliver a slide presentation. Also useful for accessing web-based information such as company information or videos.

- **Projector** – used to project and enlarge images and information such as slide presentations, videos or other electronic information from a laptop. Images are projected onto a screen for attendees to view.

- **Screen** – provides a white background so that projected images are clearly visible. Screens can be portable or static.

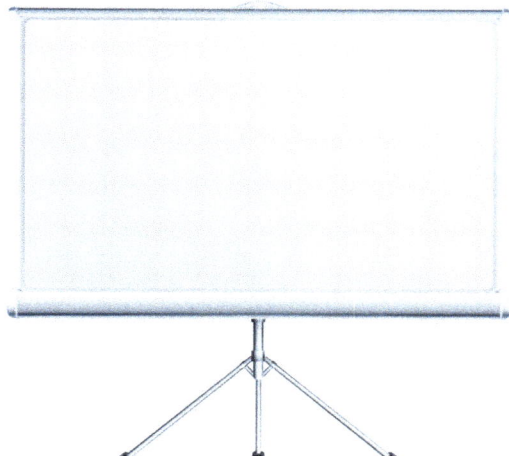

- **Stationery** – includes items such as pens, paper, flip charts, sticky notes or any other item which allows the attendee to record information, complete feedback forms or participate in practical activities.

Always find out what equipment a venue can provide for your event

> **Practise**
>
> Think about an event you have recently attended at work or as part of your social life. This could be a team meeting, a careers event or a course lesson.
>
> 1. Make a list of all the equipment and resources used by the organisation and presenters during the event.
> 2. Were you provided with any equipment or resources? If so, what were they for?

Information requirements also need to be prepared in advance. Event materials may be varied and extensive, depending on the nature of the topic, how much information is being presented and whether the presenting organisation wants participants to have information to take away for future reference.

Link it up

Go to the 'Provide administrative support to a business event in accordance with business needs' section later in this unit for more detail on event information requirements.

Arranging visiting speakers or presenters

Speakers and presenters can add to the success of an event. Arranging speakers or presenters who are internal or external to the organisation requires planning to ensure they will add to the message being delivered. Speakers and presenters are often selected based on what they know or what they can do, but their ability to connect with the audience and engage them with the topic is just as important.

The key steps to take when arranging visiting speakers or presenters are shown in Figure 4.8.

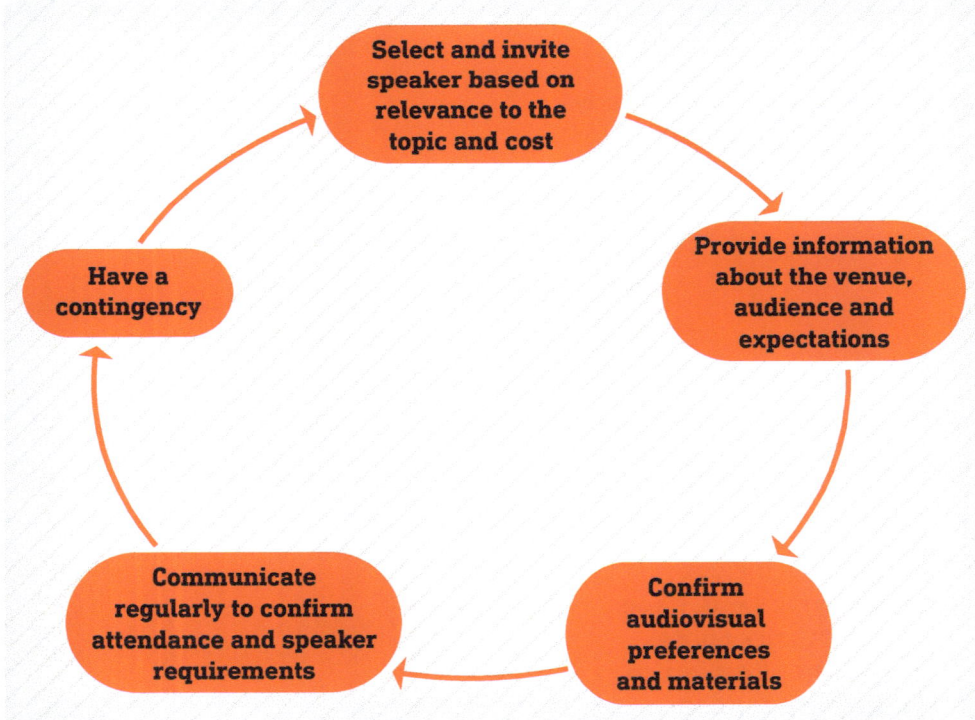

Figure 4.8: The five steps involved in booking event speakers

UNIT 4 | PLANNING, ORGANISING AND SUPPORTING BUSINESS EVENTS

Setting up the venue

Certain room layouts work particularly well with different types of events. Figure 4.9 is a guide to common event room layouts.

Room layouts

Classroom	Conference	U-Shape
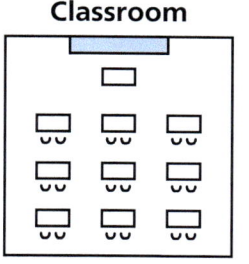		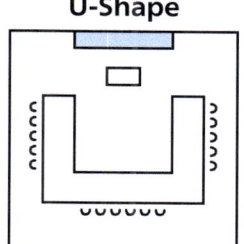
Suitable for small to medium groups of people sat in ones or twos.	Classic centrally positioned table, suitable for discussion and maintaining eye contact with all participants.	Suitable for presentations led from the front. Allows all participants to view a screen or presenter and encourages discussion.
Type of event Teaching, training or exams	**Type of event** Small meeting	**Type of event** Presentation, training or demonstration
Theatre	Fishbone	Banquet
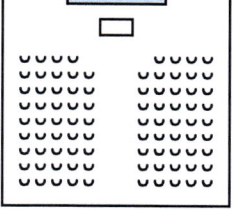	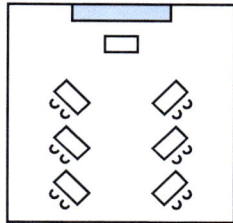	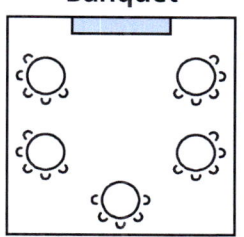
Suitable for optimising the number of participants. Used mainly for viewing a screen or listening to presenters.	Similar to a classroom layout but with tables angled towards the centre, which is more conducive to discussion.	Tables around the outside of the room, suitable for seating groups of people or group activities.
Type of event Product launch, presentation or display	**Type of event** Informal tuition or work area	**Type of event** Dinner dance, entertainment or workshop

Figure 4.9: Typical layouts for an event room

Think about the different layouts you have experienced in different types of lessons. How effective did you find each layout and why?

Practise

Using the information about room layouts in Figure 4.9, have a go at setting out different room layouts using the tables and chairs in your work area. Arrange equipment and lay out resources and materials for participants.

Setting up equipment

Once the room layout is arranged, you will need to arrange the equipment, check it is functioning correctly and provide the resources and materials for participants to use. A **RISK ASSESSMENT** of the room will also need to be completed.

143

Refreshments

Unless an event is very brief, participants will expect the event hosts to provide refreshments. The event budget will determine the type and amount of refreshments an organisation provides; however, as a minimum, drinking water should be supplied.

Refreshments may include:

- **hot and cold drinks** – including tea, coffee and hot chocolate or canned drinks, fruit juice or squash
- **biscuits and pastries** – served with hot drinks during planned breaks in proceedings and bought fresh on the morning of the event
- **fruit** – a healthy alternative for those who prefer a lower fat and sugar option. Fruit which doesn't create too much mess, such as apples or grapes, is most popular
- **boiled sweets** – served in bowls on tables and available throughout the event. Sweets provide that essential boost of sugar required to keep participants alert
- **hot and cold snacks** – common at all-day events and also offered as a lunch option in a self-serve buffet.

Once you have worked out what to serve event participants, you need to confirm how this will be served. Depending on the event location and any additional service agreements made with the venue, refreshments will either be served by the venue or your organisation. Some venues provide break out rooms where refreshments are served and to provide participants with an opportunity to stretch their legs away from the confines of the event room.

Common types of refreshment service are shown in Table 4.4.

Table 4.4: Types of refreshment service

Service	Description
Self-service	Refreshments are laid out in a suitable and accessible location for participants to help themselves. This may also include vending machines.
Assisted service	Service staff serve participants refreshments in a given location away from the event location, such as a break out room.
Table service	Participants are served refreshments in the event or meeting room.

If the organisation is providing the resources, equipment and resources will be needed to prepare refreshments for participants. Use the following checklist to ensure you have prepared everything you will need.

CHECKLIST REFRESHMENTS

- ☐ teacups and saucers or coffee cups/mugs
- ☐ coffee, teabags, sugar and sweeteners
- ☐ suitable bowls or containers for coffee etc.
- ☐ biscuits, pastries, fruit and snacks
- ☐ cutlery including teaspoons
- ☐ paper napkins
- ☐ buffet or sandwiches
- ☐ provision for waste
- ☐ kettle or tea urn
- ☐ milk and milk jug
- ☐ soft drinks and glasses
- ☐ crockery including side plates

Rules, regulations and legal requirements

Rules and regulations are in place to protect people. When things go wrong, individuals and organisations can be held accountable for their actions. Protecting people requires planning, assessment of risk and appropriate action to be taken to prevent risks, hazards and non-compliance.

When preparing for an event, you must consider the following areas.

Health and safety
- access and unobstructed walkways and exits
- evacuation routes and assembly points
- how to raise the alarm
- risk assessment of rooms
- whether equipment is safe and in good working order
- smoking policies and designated smoking areas (on- or off-site)
- accident reporting procedures
- location of first aid box and responsible person/first aider
- heating, lighting and ventilation

Food safety
- checking food allergies and dietary requirements of attendees
- preparing, cooking, serving and storing food correctly
- checking food items are fresh and in date
- maintaining standards of personal hygiene including hand washing

Spectator or crowd safety
- licensed and trained security personnel
- maximum room or venue capacity
- sufficient basic facilities such as drinking water, toilets and exits

Activities that require a temporary event licence
- selling or serving alcohol
- age restricted sales, e.g. alcohol and tobacco
- providing entertainment
- serving hot food or drink between 11.00 p.m. and 5.00 a.m.
- fewer than 500 attendees
- lasting no more than seven days.

To ensure the event is **COMPLIANT**, organisations must take the appropriate measures depending on the nature of the event. **PRECAUTIONARY** measures are measures taken in advance to protect against possible danger or failure. **PREVENTATIVE** measures are used to prevent or hinder an unwanted occurrence. These may include:

- size and location
- whether the event is held indoors or outdoors
- characteristics of the audience e.g. age, numbers and supervision ratios
- whether contractors or traders are present
- any special effects, for example fireworks.

What if...?

You have organised an event and one of the attendees raises the alarm that a fire has been lit in the men's toilets. How would you handle this situation? Considerations should include:

1 remaining calm
2 calling emergency services
3 efficient and safe evacuation of participants
4 location of assembly points
5 checking that all participants are accounted for
6 reporting injuries.

Expect the unexpected

Events can be complex with many areas which could potentially fail. Knowing what these are and how to deal with them if they occur will ensure you can react quickly and appropriately, ensuring the event continues to run smoothly and to time.

The types of problems which may occur, their causes and appropriate contingencies are shown in Table 4.5.

Table 4.5: Possible problems, causes and contingencies

Potential failure	Possible cause	Contingency
Audiovisual equipment	Equipment fault	Spare audiovisual equipment and cables
	Electrical or Bluetooth connectivity fault	Contact details for technical support
	Missing cables or components	Have presentation slides as paper copies
Late or cancelled speakers	Unforeseen delays	Ask other guests or colleagues to present
	Illness or injury	Continue with other **AGENDA** items
	Higher priority, last-minute commitments	
Event staff in the wrong location or missing	Confusion over timings or responsibilities	Have a person who moves around the event to identify and resolve issues as they arise
	Being treated for an injury	Allow dedicated time for breaks
	Taking an unplanned comfort break	Have more staff than you think you need
Materials not arriving	Delay in production	Take a USB flash drive containing the resources and print on-site
	Lost in the post	

This information should form part of your contingency plan. This is a separate document to your event plan. You never know when you or your colleagues involved in the event will need to use it.

A4 Processing and communicating information required before and during the event

Business events are all about information to be communicated to others. Information needs to be processed before it can be communicated. There are many different information processing and communication activities which need to be completed, both before the event takes place and during the event. In this section we will explore information and communication requirements.

> **Link it up**
>
> Go to Unit 3 to find out more information about processing and communicating information.

Information requirements

Examples of information requirements are shown in Figure 4.10.

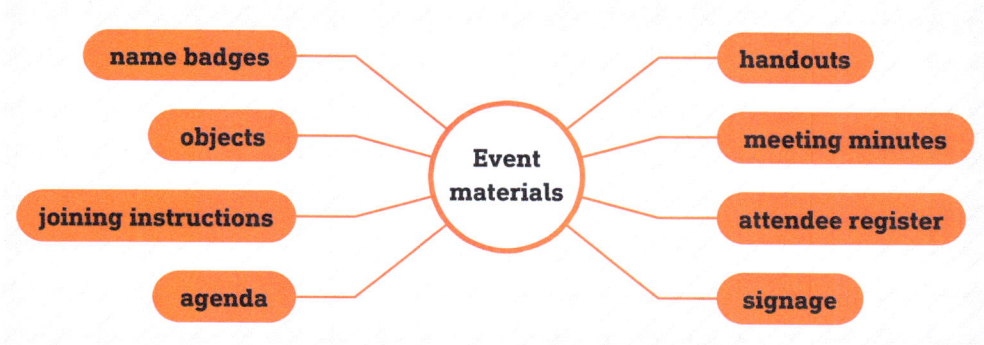

Figure 4.10: Information requirements

- **Agenda** – a list of meeting or event proceedings, including timings and person(s) responsible
- **Meeting minutes** – records from the last meeting or event for the purpose of agreeing and signing off action points or decisions
- **Joining instructions** – information given to attendees relating to the location and how to get there, for example, transport options, registration procedures, teleconference or webinar joining codes and information about the venue
- **Attendee register** – names and contact details for all confirmed attendees
- **Name badges** – wearable badges, lanyards, clips or pins, table place cards
- **Signage** – organisation marketing signage, directions to the venue, seating plan
- **Handouts** – copies of presentation slides, reference materials, worksheets and exercise materials
- **Objects** – physical items relevant to the meeting which may include organisational products and teambuilding activity tools.

Methods of publicising an event

An event will not be successful if the intended audience does not turn up. How can you raise awareness of an event to ensure maximum attendance? The method of publicising the event will largely depend on the nature of the event and whether it is internal or external to the organisation.

Before publicising an event or sending invitations, you must establish and confirm the key information, as shown in Figure 4.11. Refer to the agreed event brief to establish these information requirements.

Figure 4.11: An example of a publicised event

Workplaces typically **PUBLICISE** (make public, announce) events using different types of business technology. Technology should be selected based on its suitability to process or share information relating to the event, and may include:

- **social media networks** – an efficient tool to publicise an event to a mass audience; typically used for events external to the organisation. Facebook and Twitter provide integrated functions to create events. LinkedIn can also be used to communicate directly with the target audience. However, this method will only reach those who follow the organisation on social media networks.
- **calendar invites** – integrated within organisational email software. It allows the organiser to invite participants to an event at a specific time and location and has integrated response tools which ask participants to confirm their attendance. Once confirmed, events are automatically added to the participant's calendar. Software also allows event materials, such as the agenda, to be attached to the invitation.
- **email** – used for informal meetings with few participants, such as one-to-one or small team meetings. Organisations may also use email to share adverts for larger events containing images and graphics.

Practise

Try producing an advertisement or email communication about a personal event you have coming up. The communication should be aimed at your friends, relatives or sports team and should:

1. include What, Why, When, Where and Who

2. be produced in an interesting way so that the reader's eyes are drawn to its content, such as use of bold colours, images or tag lines.

Carrying out relevant administrative activities

Processing and communicating information requires a range of administrative skills to ensure information is entered, edited, checked, printed, collated and shared with others.

Table 4.6 shows a range of administrative activities typically associated with event preparation and the types of tasks which you may be required to complete.

Producing documents	Photocopying	Collating documents	Responding to email queries
Agenda	Meeting minutes	Binding participant packs	Duration of event
Invitation or advert	Handouts	Stapling minutes	Venue queries
Presentation slides	Worksheets	Guillotine business cards	Confirming attendance
Participant pack	Signage	Laminating name badges	Responding to suppliers
Joining instructions	Evaluation forms	Sharing information online	Briefing presenters

Table 4.6: Tasks to complete when preparing for an event

Preparing and distributing participant packs

The participant pack is one of the most important documents as it provides all the necessary information, instructions and activities a participant will need. Packs will vary depending on the nature of the event and the level of participant engagement.

Common contents of a participant pack may include:
- **front cover** – event or business meeting title or objective
- **welcome statement** – includes a statement from the host of the event such as the Managing Director, information about the content of the event, start and finish times and registration arrangements
- **agenda** – order of event proceedings including details of presenters and break room locations
- **venue information** – including location, contact details, facilities and emergency procedures
- **travel instructions** – including full address and postcode of the venue, any satellite navigation considerations, how to get to the venue using different modes of transport and where to park on arrival
- **accommodation arrangements** – check in and check out arrangements, cloakroom or bag drop facilities, breakfast service times and room locations
- **slide presentation handouts** – printed from the original slide presentation and containing space for participants to record notes
- **reference materials** – information for participants to have in advance of the event or to refer to afterwards. These may include pre-reading requirements, organisational statistical reports or revisions to policies or procedures

Link it up

Go to Unit 2 to find more information about providing administrative services and using different items of office equipment.

Link it up

Go to Unit 3 for more information about business technology, application software and web-based systems and technology.

- **activity sheets** – may include worksheets, scenarios for group activities, assessment questions or other relevant information to be used in event activities.

It is worth remembering that the participant information may not necessarily be produced as a pack of paper documents; it may be communicated and shared electronically through web-based technology, such as online collaboration software.

Think about the most appropriate format for sharing information: electronically or on paper?

Achieving maximum attendance

When planning and organising business events, it is important to ensure attendance is maximised and there is a positive response to the event itself. Maximising attendance will prevent the need for any repeat or **MOP UP EVENTS** (events which take place after the main event for the benefit of participants who couldn't attend the first time). This will save time and money.

Steps to achieve maximum attendance

Positive and proactive steps can be taken to maximise attendance. These include:

- sending out invitations early to encourage participants to prioritise the event
- personalising invitations and event correspondence to make participants feel they are personally required to attend the event
- reviewing participant acceptances and using follow-up phone calls and email to check attendance
- providing full and accurate information to participants
- optimising publicity of the event using a range of methods including social media networks
- asking attendees and presenters to promote the event
- including breaks and fun time in the agenda
- selecting a venue and location which meets requirements of all participants
- organising and supporting the event in a manner which presents a positive impression of the organisation to participants.

> **Skills and knowledge check**
>
> ☐ I can source a suitable venue and make arrangements for business travel and accommodation.
> ☐ I can organise people, equipment, resources and event materials.
> ☐ I can produce and send event-related information to participants in advance.
> ☐ I have practised setting up different venue room layouts.
>
> ○ I can describe the key features of an event plan.
> ○ I know what is meant by a contingency plan.
> ○ I know why agreeing an event brief is important and what is included.
> ○ I can identify different types of business events and meetings.

B Provide administrative support to a business event in accordance with business needs

B1 Welcoming and registering event participants

The welcome and registration process may be the participants' first face-to-face interaction with the organisation and their first impression of how efficient and friendly the staff are. This should fill the participant with confidence that the event they are attending will be well organised and efficiently run.

Greeting event participants

Protocols for greeting event participants on arrival may vary for different organisations; however, the objectives remain the same:

- Greeting participants in a warm, friendly and professional manner, and using positive **BODY LANGUAGE** will make participants feel valued and appreciated.
- Applying **INTERPERSONAL SKILLS** (skills relating to the communication and interaction between people) and being approachable will demonstrate your ability to form positive working relationships.

How you greet participants is important

Practise

Turn to a fellow student and practise greeting each other. Use positive and friendly verbal and non-verbal communication skills to show that you are pleased to welcome them to the organisation. Repeat this exercise using a negative and unfriendly approach. Don't forget to incorporate body language into how you communicate!

1. How did you feel when you were greeted in a positive manner? How did being greeted in a negative manner make you feel? Compare your feelings after the two interactions.

2. What impression would you get of the organisation based on the type of greeting you receive?

Personal behaviours and presentation

It is extremely important to demonstrate appropriate personal behaviours and presentation during all interactions with event participants; otherwise participants will find the event memorable for all the wrong reasons! It is essential to familiarise yourself with the behaviours expected of you by the business and to observe how other colleagues demonstrate them. Examples of appropriate personal behaviours and presentation are described in Table 4.7.

Behaviour	Description
Professionalism	Professionalism includes how you act around participants, how you communicate, your attitude towards work and people, your appearance and how knowledgeable and confident you are.
Politeness and courtesy	Demonstrate good manners and use considerate behaviours. Address participants appropriately or, where possible, greet them by their first name (or last name if more appropriate).
Good customer service	Take an interest in participants without discussing their personal lives too much. Finding out a little about them will strengthen the relationship and may help you to further understand their needs and expectations. Demonstrate a positive and helpful attitude, communicate accurate information clearly and aim to respond to queries, problems and complaints quickly. Participants will respond well to staff who are conscientious and motivated, keen to help and enthusiastic about the organisation.

Table 4.7: Appropriate behaviours when interacting with event participants

Recording attendance of participants and issuing name badges

Why could it be important to record who has attended the event? Why is this information needed?

> **What if...?**
>
> You have organised an event and one of the attendees discovers a fire in a supplies room, which is spreading quickly. The alarm is raised and participants are asked to evacuate to the assembly point using the nearest exit.
>
> 1 How will you know if all staff and participants have evacuated safely?
>
> 2 What are the implications of sending emergency services into a dangerous situation without knowing whether anyone is left in the building?

In addition to being needed in emergencies, attendance records are often used for other organisational purposes:

- When staff have attended training or received key information, this should be added to Human Resources (HR) or operational records.
- Attendance at events may attract payments or incentives; having this information means the participant gets paid or receives the necessary incentive.
- Information can be used to update Customer Relationship Management information systems. These are databases which record existing customers, those who have left and potential new customers. This information can be used to follow up on business leads or send marketing information about products and services.
- Event organisers will quickly find out if individual participants are attending who are required to take calls or need to respond to urgent situations.
- Information can be used to split the participants for the purpose of smaller group activities.

Name badges

Issuing name badges can have many benefits other than identifying the participant to others at the event. Benefits include:

- confirming identification of the participants where photographs are included
- distinguishing participants from event staff
- identifying the role and organisation of the participant
- allowing participants to put faces to names
- providing opportunities for participants to network.

Name badges should contain more than just the name of the participant; this should be considered when preparing name badges for an event. An example of a name badge is shown in Figure 4.12.

Figure 4.12: An example of a name badge

During planning, you should have considered how participants will wear their name badges. This will allow you to provide necessary fixings such as pins, clips or **LANYARDS** (a cord that allows you to wear your name badge around your neck).

Meeting the needs of participants

Participants attending the event may have many different needs and expectations, as shown in Figure 4.13. Although it may be impossible to meet all the needs of all the participants, you should try to meet most of them, and where this is not possible, provide reasons for not doing so.

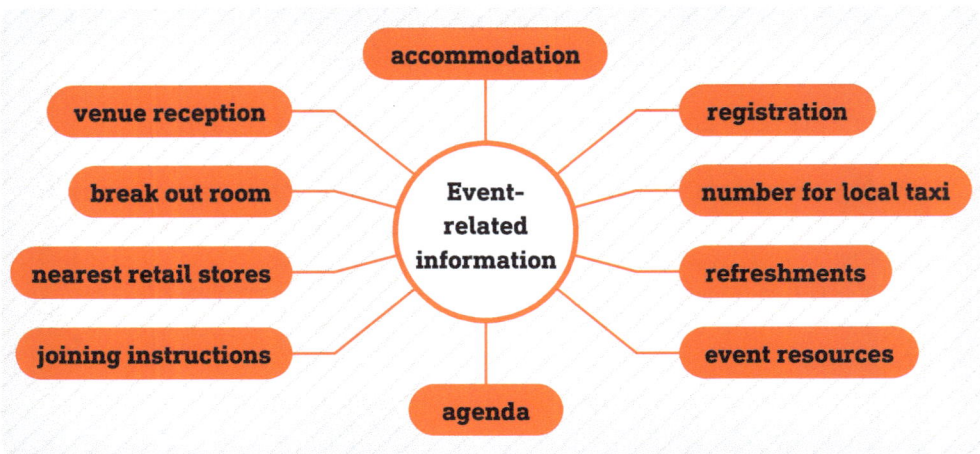

Figure 4.13: Event-related information

It will be helpful for you to arrive early or visit the venue in advance, to find out about:

- venue room plan and building layout, including emergency exits and assembly points
- the location of facilities such as toilets, restaurant, luggage storage and meeting rooms
- venue Wi-Fi access codes and procedures
- local amenities such as shops, banks, train stations and bus stops, local taxi firms and numbers
- procedures for entering or exiting secure car parks, including passcodes
- check-in and check-out times of accommodation.

Having this information before participants arrive will minimise delays when these questions are asked. It will also give participants the impression you are organised and knowledgeable.

Individual participant needs

It is important to have knowledge of the protected characteristics within the Equality Act when meeting the needs of individuals. DISCRIMINATION (treating someone differently) is unlawful on many grounds.

It is important to consider the civersity of the population in the UK

All participants have a legal right to be treated equally and fairly irrespective of their protected characteristic. However, some groups have specific needs that will need to be met by event staff. Table 4.8 shows examples of these groups, their individual needs and how these needs can be met.

Table 4.8: Meeting the needs of participants with protected characteristics

Protected characteristic	Participant	How to meet individual participant needs
Age	Elderly	• Seating in break out rooms and common areas • Assistance carrying bags • Assistance with steps
Disability	Visual, hearing and mobility disabilities	• Wheelchair access including ramps and wide-frame doorways • Ground floor facilities or lift access to upper floors • Toilet facilities with grab rails and lower level sinks and driers • Making resources available through hearing aid induction loops, large print and braille • Consideration for text and page colours of event resources • Providing desks at wheelchair height
Pregnancy and maternity	Pregnant women	• Seating in break out rooms and common areas • Assistance carrying bags
	Parent and baby	• Quiet location or designated space for breastfeeding • Facilities for warming milk • Baby changing facilities • Pram access including ramps and wide-frame doorways • Crèche facilities
Religion or belief	Any participants	• Quiet location or designated space for prayer • Food preparation, storage and service considerations which respect religious beliefs/customs such as Ramadan and halal or kosher food laws • Consideration for participant dress
Race	Non-English speaking	• Speaking clearly and slowly using simple language and short sentences • Having versions of resources in different languages • Having colleagues available who speak other languages

Communicating effectively with participants and support staff

Communicating effectively is vital to the success of an event. Communication involves both verbal and non-verbal communication.

Verbal communication
- Use appropriate greetings such as 'good morning' or 'how may I help you?'
- Speak clearly using language that the participant will understand, avoiding **JARGON**.
- Use an appropriate **TONE OF VOICE** which considers who you are speaking to and how you speak.
- Don't speak too loudly, but also make sure you can be heard.
- Adjust the language you use and the speed you speak at if customers do not speak English as their first language.

Non-verbal communication
- Smile at the participant and appear approachable.
- Make eye contact with participants and look at them when you are talking to them.
- Use open body language e.g. don't cross your arms or put your hands in your pockets.
- Use facial expressions that make you look approachable. Look as if you want to help and show you are paying attention.

Providing refreshments to meet the needs of participants

Refreshments may be provided to participants on arrival, at agreed breaks and during the lunchbreak. You will need to know the timings of these breaks to ensure refreshments are ready as soon as the break begins. Breaks are often only 10–15 minutes long, so plan carefully to ensure participants have an opportunity to get refreshments before the next part of the event.

> **Practise**
>
> Try taking a refreshments order from a group to see if you can (a) get it right and (b) meet everyone's individual preferences such as:
>
> 1 tea, coffee, hot chocolate or cold drink
> 2 how much sugar or how many sweeteners they take
> 3 how strong they like their tea or coffee
> 4 whether they prefer whole, semi-skimmed, skimmed or lactose-free milk.
>
> After you have taken the group's refreshments order, are you able to remember who ordered what?

Once participants are refreshed, cups and other items will need to be collected and arrangements should be made for these to be washed and put away or returned clean to the refreshment area. For plastic or paper cups, they will need to put in the appropriate bins. Replenishment of stocks including milk and biscuits is also required.

Participant dietary requirements

People may be intolerant to various food items or they could be making life decisions about their diet based on medical advice. They may also have a preference, or have religious or moral beliefs, leading to specific dietary needs. Some of the most common dietary requirements are shown in Table 4.9.

Table 4.9: Possible dietary requirements of participants

Requirement	Description
Vegetarian	A person who does not eat meat or fish, and sometimes other animal products, especially for moral, religious, or health reasons.
Vegan	A person who does not eat or use animal products.
Gluten-free	Gluten is the protein found in wheat and therefore products which contain wheat. These include bread, pasta and flour.
Food allergy	There are many different food allergies. Two of the most common food allergies are to nuts and dairy products. A dairy-free diet requires lactose-free drinks and meals. A nut allergy is difficult to manage as there are nuts contained in foods you wouldn't expect, including chocolate products.
Halal	Halal relates to meat products which are permitted, lawful and allowed to be eaten according to Islamic law.
Kosher	Food, or premises in which food is sold, cooked, or eaten, which satisfies the requirements of Jewish law.

> **Link it up**
>
> Go to the Ready for assessment section in this unit, 'Making preparations for an event in line with agreed brief', for further information about refreshments.

Information relating to dietary requirements needs to be obtained in advance to allow caterers to accommodate these needs. Food containing allergens such as nuts must be labelled clearly.

Health, safety and security monitoring

During the course of the event, it is most important to monitor health, safety and security of people, property and premises. This is to ensure that any compliance issues or factors that may affect the comfort and protection of participants are identified and resolved before they have a significant impact on the event.

Most health, safety and security requirements can be observed or indeed experienced by support staff, who are then in a position to respond quickly. These include:

- Participants' arrival and departure:
  - issuing participant cards
  - signing participants in and out
- Temperature:
  - too warm or too cold
- Lighting:
  - sun streaming through windows
  - poor or bright internal lighting
  - glare on screens
  - poor projection of presentation
- Ventilation:
  - too stuffy
  - draughts from open doors or windows
- Valuable or important items being left unattended:
  - personal belongings
  - event equipment and technology
  - confidential or commercially sensitive information
- Evacuation procedures compromised:
  - exit and access routes blocked
  - faulty fire protection equipment
  - missing or unclear emergency evacuation procedures
- Information security:
  - personal or commercially sensitive information being stored insecurely or communicated to people who are not authorised to have it.

It is important to be vigilant when supporting a business event. Spend time 'people watching' as their body language will give you signals that they are uncomfortable.

Be aware if participants are uncomfortable

Vigilance will also be useful when identifying participants or others at the venue who are disregarding safety and security rules. Such incidents must be reported.

Familiarise yourself with venue procedures for opening and closing windows, doors and blinds, and altering heating and lighting levels. Establish what you can and can't change and where it is necessary to ask for assistance. Some venues have systems that are tricky to operate, so you may need to ask for help or expertise from the venue maintenance staff. If you do need help, establishing who you would need to ask and how to contact them should be done as soon as possible so problems are resolved quickly.

Practise

Pretend you are a delegate at a business meeting or event and you feel uncomfortable. See if other group members can work out what your needs are and how they can help. Scenarios could include:

1. being hot or cold
2. not being able to see the screen
3. feeling unwell
4. losing personal belongings
5. having the sun in your eyes
6. struggling to locate facilities.

B2 Responding to queries, issues, problems and complaints

How you deal with participant queries, issues, problems and complaints will have a direct impact on how the participant feels about the event and the organisation.

Responding to queries appropriately

There are key behaviours which can be applied to any situation involving unhappy participants, as shown in Table 4.10.

Table 4.10: How to respond helpfully to participants' queries and problems

Response/behaviour	Explanation
Communicate	Seek clarification of the issue and apply active listening skills to ensure you fully understand the nature of the issue.
Be polite	This is essential, no matter how difficult the participant may be.
Show empathy	This means showing you really understand how the participant is feeling about a problem. Offer apologies in a timely and sincere manner.
Keep participants informed	If you are dealing with a query which may take time to resolve, keep the participants informed. Even if you don't have the answer yet, you can reassure them that you are doing all you can to help them.
Don't disagree	It is important to be tactful, even if you think the participant is wrong. Focus on the issue, not the opinion. If the situation becomes difficult, call for assistance.
Use appropriate body language	Making eye contact gives the participant positive signals that you are interested in helping them.
Resolve promptly	Make the participant's query, issue, problem or complaint your priority and look to resolve it as quickly as you can.
Escalate the problem	Recognise where your skills, experience or level of authority will limit your ability to resolve the problem and seek assistance from your supervisor, event manager or venue staff.

Practise

Think about four difficult but realistic queries, issues, problems or complaints you might have to deal with at a business event. For each example consider the following questions.

1. What is the nature of the query, issue, problem or complaint?
2. How would you respond to the participant?
3. How would you resolve the query, issue, problem or complaint?
4. What impact will this have on the participant if not resolved?

Potential queries, issues, problems and complaints

The types of queries, issues, problems and complaints may differ depending on the nature of the event, the needs of the participant and how well organised the event is. Here are some examples of common event-related scenarios and how you might resolve them.

- Event finishing late:
  - Designate a timekeeper to track timeliness of agenda items and flag up where items run over.
  - Place important topics which require more discussion at the top of the agenda.
  - Start promptly.
  - Advise that questions will be answered at the end of the agenda.
- Dominant participants:
  - Don't be afraid to ask a participant to allow others to speak.
  - Agree to discuss further after the event.
- Locating and accessing facilities:
  - Have pre-prepared information to hand, such as maps and transport information.
  - Ask participants if they require transport such as taxis and book this in advance.
- Delays due to equipment failure:
  - Set activities that do not require equipment, such as practical exercises and discussions.
  - Use **BACK-UP** equipment or obtain technical support quickly.
- Content doesn't meet the needs of participants:
  - Practise presentation of the materials in advance of the event and seek feedback on whether the content is fit for purpose and meets event objectives.
- Late or absent participants:
  - Agree to fill in missed agenda items after the event.
  - Have a contingency for others to fill in where participants are contributing to the event agenda.
- Unprofessional or unhelpful attitude, behaviour or service of event or venue staff:
  - Agree in advance the level of service expected of event staff.
  - Report complaints to the event co-ordinator or manager.
- Inadequate or poorly maintained facilities:
  - Speak to venue staff to rectify problems quickly.
- Health, safety or security problems:
  - Report to event manager or venue staff.
  - Restrict access to the location or equipment until it is made safe.

B3 Taking and distributing minutes

Whether the meeting is a formal, informal or business event, you will need to document proceedings so your organisation has a record of discussions, outcomes and agreed actions. In most cases, this record will be in the form of minutes.

The minute-taker should not be an active participant in the meeting as it is difficult to contribute to discussions and make accurate notes at the same time.

Different types of minutes

How you produce minutes and the information required will depend on the type of meeting. Some common types of minutes and when they can be used are shown in Table 4.11.

Table 4.11: Types of minutes

Resolution	Narrative	Action
Usually recorded in formal meetings such as board meetings. They include actions and resolutions agreed by organisation directors.	Usually recorded during meetings where detail and context are required. This may be an interview or investigation.	Usually generated where the focus of the meeting is to produce an action plan. This could be a team meeting or a project planning meeting.

The minute taker's responsibilities include activities before and after the meeting or event, as well as in the meeting itself, as shown in Figure 4.14.

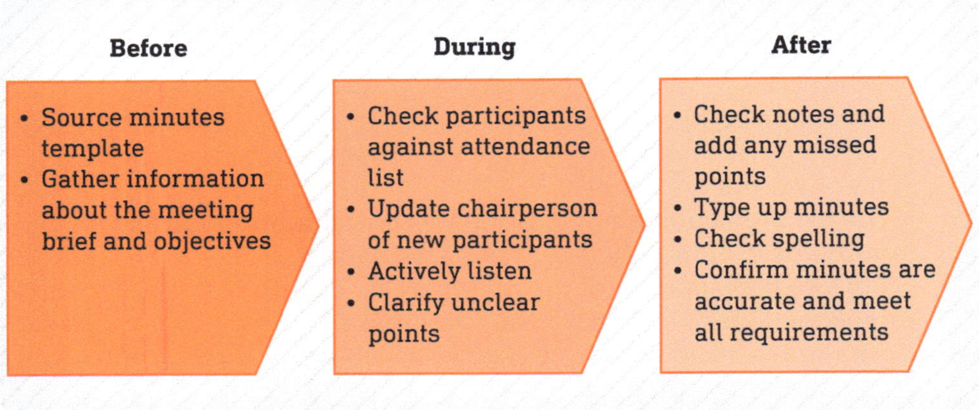

Before
- Source minutes template
- Gather information about the meeting brief and objectives

During
- Check participants against attendance list
- Update chairperson of new participants
- Actively listen
- Clarify unclear points

After
- Check notes and add any missed points
- Type up minutes
- Check spelling
- Confirm minutes are accurate and meet all requirements

Figure 4.14: Minute-taking process

Applying good practice

The notes you take must accurately reflect the meeting or event you are recording minutes for. There are important aspects of minute writing which need to be taken into consideration:

- **format** – formats may include written, audio or video
- **structure** – MOTIONS (formal proposals put to a meeting), additional notes, key points, recommendations, agreed decisions and actions
- **content** – location, date and time of meeting, persons present, apologies from absent participants, agreement of previous minutes, review of actions previously agreed, new discussion points and actions, any other business, information about PROXY VOTERS (meeting members who may delegate their voting powers to others at the meeting), confirmation of QUORUM (the minimum number of members that must be present to make the proceedings of the meeting valid), motions passed, resolutions agreed, voting outcomes, names of nominator and seconder
- **use of professional language, tone and grammar** – use past tense, limit the use of the passive voice, write in the third person, use business terminology and accepted language and grammar.

> **Practise**
>
> Can you identify what is wrong with the following extract from a meeting minutes?
>
> Address the following areas.
>
> 1 Spelling, punctuation and grammar
> 2 Language and tone
> 3 Professionalism
> 4 Valid and relevant content.
>
> > **It was agreed that the business should open late once a week to so more customer can visit the store. Abbie says she doesn't want to work late as she has kids but says that Justin and Tina should go as their single.**

Storing and distributing meeting minutes

Typically, minutes should be distributed within one week of the meeting. Minutes should be:

- checked and approved by the **CHAIRPERSON** before they are shared with participants
- changed where requested by the chairperson
- circulated by post or email to all those present at the meeting, those who sent apologies and anyone who needs to receive a copy for information.

The Companies Act 2006 requires organisations to keep 'proper records' of meetings where business decisions are made by members or directors. These records provide evidence of how the business makes decisions and the actions taken to resolve business issues, so they are considered a **LEGAL DOCUMENT**.

These records will be examined in the event of:

- a business dispute with staff, suppliers or customers
- a need to make sure the organisation has completed the necessary checks around health, safety and security of people, premises and information.

It is also a legal requirement for company records to be kept for ten years following the date of the meeting. Records should be kept in a secure location in storage media that is appropriate and that will not destroyed, removed or lost. After this time, records may be destroyed using an appropriate and secure method.

Skills and knowledge check

- ☐ I have practised processing and communicating different types of event information.
- ☐ I have practised welcoming participants using professional behaviours and communication skills.
- ☐ I can provide refreshments to participants in accordance with their preferences and dietary requirements.

- ○ I know what actions to take to ensure an event runs smoothly and attendance is maximised.
- ○ I know what types of queries, issues and complaints I might face and how to effectively resolve them.
- ○ I know how to check that necessary health and safety and any legal, local and contractual requirements have been met.
- ○ I know what needs to be included in meeting minutes and how to record them accurately.

C Carry out follow-up activities after a business event

C1 Follow-up activities to an event

After any good party or event, there will be the need to clear up and carry out post-event actions, whether this is paying for the room or DJ or sending thank you cards. The same principles apply to business meetings and events.

Carrying out post-event and follow-up actions

Activities are broken down into two defined categories.

Post-event activities

These are activities that need to take place immediately after the event and are generally carried out on the same day or very soon after. Activities may include:

- paying the venue and/or suppliers for goods and services
- clearing up the room, including putting tables and chairs back in their normal position
- disconnecting and returning IT equipment such as projector, screen, laptop and other resources
- clearing cups, glasses and other resources relating to refreshments
- collecting participant materials which have been left behind or are spare
- circulating post-event information such as minutes or other agreed information
- collecting feedback from participants.

Follow-up activities

These are activities which may take some time to complete in response to meeting actions or in line with your agreed responsibilities and objectives. Activities may include:
- planning and organising follow-up or the next meeting or event
- analysing feedback from participants and sharing results.

Evaluating the performance of external services

For a business, there are many reasons why it is important to review the quality of external services during the course of your event. External services may include the venue, supplier of refreshments or presenter.

It has always been important to measure the impact of external services on the event and the organisation. In this economic age, organisations need to ensure they receive value for money when running events.

Identifying where external services haven't been delivered in line with agreed expectations provides opportunities to negotiate better deals or explore alternatives.

> **Link it up**
>
> Go to the Ready for assessment section in this unit, 'Making preparations for an event in line with agreed brief', for further information about payment terms and conditions when booking venues.

Use feedback to improve performance

Author Ray Carter developed an effective model for evaluating service providers and suppliers called the ten Cs model.
1. **Competency** – Did they demonstrate the ability to meet the needs of your organisation and event requirements?
2. **Capacity** – Did they have enough time and resources to handle your event requirements?
3. **Commitment** – Have they demonstrated a commitment to delivering high quality products and services?

4. **Control** – How much control did they have over policies, processes and procedures?
5. **Cash** – Are they in financial good health and able to absorb uncertainties in the economic climate?
6. **Cost** – How did the cost of their products and/or services compare with those of other similar companies?
7. **Consistency** – Were products and services delivered to a consistent standard?
8. **Culture** – Were the organisational cultures of service providers and suppliers aligned with those of your organisation?
9. **Clean** – Do they have a commitment to sustainability and the environment?
10. **Communication** – How effective was communication from them, including keeping you advised of progress or delays?

A simpler way to evaluate the performance of external suppliers is to measure their **service, efficiency, quality** and **reliability**.

Collecting feedback from event participants

The purpose of collecting feedback is primarily to identify how to make future events a better experience for the participant. It is important to agree feedback objectives which state what the organisation is looking to achieve by gathering and using comments from participants. So, what kind of information would it be helpful to collect? Examples are shown in Figure 4.15.

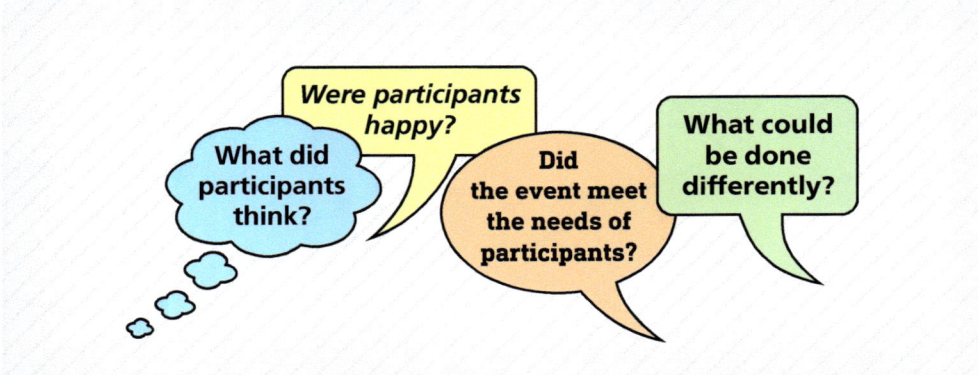

Figure 4.15: Examples of useful information for feedback

This information can have a positive and far-reaching impact on the organisation, including:
- improving the planning, preparation and delivery of future events
- measuring participant satisfaction
- creating a better participant experience
- delivering information in a more engaging and interesting way
- improving business relationships
- increasing attendance.

There are many ways of collecting feedback from event participants. Methods which work well for your organisation may not suit others; therefore it is important to consider the most efficient way of capturing the information you need. Typically, event participants are asked to complete an evaluation form before they leave; however, this may not be feasible at larger events. Some methods of collecting participant feedback are shown in Table 4.12.

Feedback type	Collection method
Verbal	Customer interactions, face-to-face participant interviews or telephone interviews
Written	Questionnaires completed on the day, postal questionnaires, complaints cards, sticky note feedback
Digital	Online reviews of events and venues, online questionnaires, social media comments and posts, text messages, email, participant contact forms

Table 4.12: Different ways of collecting feedback

Figure 4.16 shows some examples of the types of questions and response formats that could be used to collect participant feedback.

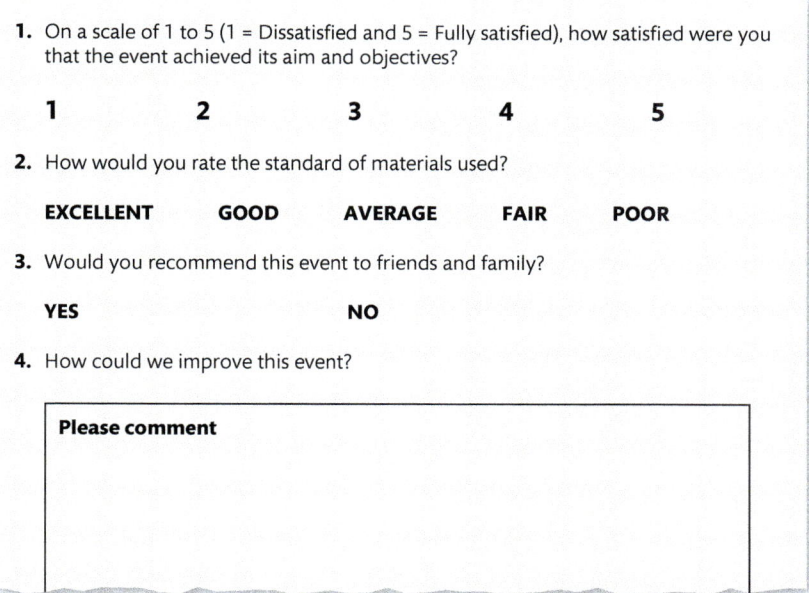

Figure 4.16: Feedback form example

Analysing participant feedback and sharing results

There are different techniques which can be used to analyse information gathered from participants. The technique used will depend on whether the organisation wants to look at all feedback, sample feedback or group feedback based on the type of participant.

Data analysis techniques may include:
- functional analysis to identify target markets, including demographic and geographic information
- statistical analysis including mean, mode, median, range and percentages
- identification of patterns and trends
- descriptive statistics including the use of tables, dashboard summaries, charts and other visual elements.

Use of basic descriptive statistics

Descriptive statistics relate to mathematical calculations that can be carried out using the information gained from event participants. This works particularly well when feedback is captured as a rating scale or a score, as shown in Table 4.13.

Table 4.13: Descriptive statistics

Statistic	Example
Mean (average)	• Average age of participants • Total age of all participants / number of participants = average age of participants
Mode (most frequently occurring)	• Main reason for complaint • Look for complaints and see which topic participants have mentioned the most
Median (middle number or response)	• Median customer score for a question • Sort results into numerical or rating group order, count up all responses and identify which one is in the middle • If there was an equal number of possible responses (e.g. 0, 1, 2, 3, 4, 5 = 6 responses), there will be two median values
Range (highest minus lowest)	• Age range of participants • Highest participant age – lowest participant age = age range
Percentages (proportion)	• Percentage of participants who would recommend the event to others • Number who answered 'yes' to the question / total number of responses to the question × 100 = the percentage of participants who would recommend the event to others

Using charts and other visual elements to present information

There are many different ways to present information gained from the analysis of customer feedback. Putting this information into a visual format will allow people to identify trends and patterns more effectively and will also help the audience to understand the information that is being presented. A famous example of this can be seen during the cholera epidemic in London, 1854.

A cholera epidemic broke out in central London, taking the lives of many people in a limited area. At that time, the cause of cholera hadn't been established. Doctor John Snow could make no sense of the 83 deaths and obtained records from the General Register Office about the victims. He plotted where the deceased had lived on a map of the area and, using this visual representation, identified a water pump that seemed to be a likely cause of the outbreak. By converting the records into a visual format, Snow was able to provide detailed evidence about the possible cause of the outbreak, which gave the authorities the information they needed to take action.

This example shows that the use of visual elements can be far more effective than words or figures in interpreting information. There are many different methods of presenting information in a visual manner to help interpretation. Figure 4.17 shows a few examples of the most widely-used ways of visually displaying information.

Try creating these various types of visual elements using the software you have available ahead of time. There are plenty of online tutorials and sources of information to help if needed.

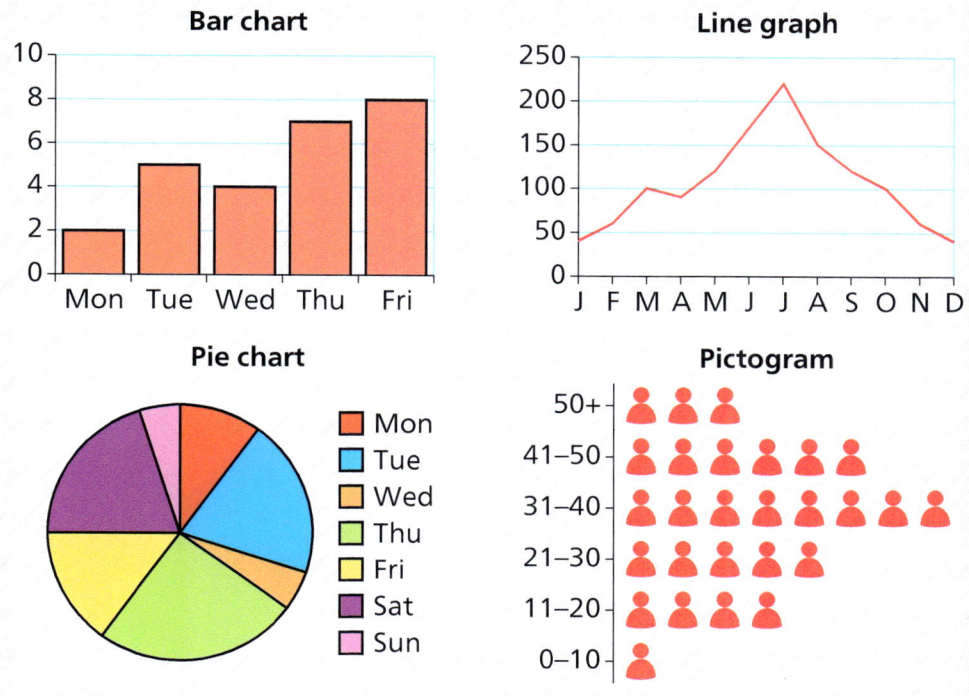

Figure 4.17: Examples of different types of graph

Patterns and trends in feedback to draw conclusions

A **PATTERN** is something that is repeated. A **TREND** is what is popular at a point in time or a change in the way people are behaving.

Identifying patterns and trends when analysing participant feedback will help an organisation to understand what participants are trying to say about the event or the organisation. Patterns in feedback may show where improvements are needed to bring up the standard or quality of an event, indicate the areas of the event which went really well or provide valuable information about ways to make the event more enjoyable or update the content.

Trends may relate to participant experiences of events inside or outside the organisation.

Before you share feedback with others, your data will need to be collated. This means providing a summary of the feedback. The best way to do this is numerically, for example:

- 69 per cent of participants were satisfied with the overall running of the event
- 72 per cent of participants would like to see more break out activities.

The most beneficial information is likely to come from negative feedback or areas where participants feel the event could be improved. Your summary information should identify these areas in a format such as bullet points.

Sharing information

You should share information in accordance with organisational procedures; however, you should try to present the data in an informative way – for example, by using graphs, charts or infographics (see Figure 4.18). This will allow you to celebrate positive feedback and communicate negative feedback as effectively as possible.

Figure 4.18: An example of an infographic

Evaluating the effectiveness of planning and arrangements

As well as gathering feedback from participants, event staff should undertake REFLECTION ACTIVITIES, identifying what went well, what went less well and how event planning, organisation and support could be better the next time around. Identifying the strengths and weaknesses of event staff and suggesting ways in which staff can improve their performance will contribute a lot to the evaluation and improvement process.

During evaluation, staff should identify what went well and less well in relation to:

- effectiveness of the event plan
- preparation activities
- organisation of information, resources and equipment
- customer service skills
- clarity and accuracy of information
- following organisational processes and procedures
- how well the event met the brief and objectives.

Future improvements

Using your own experiences and those of other staff, participants and external services, you can build a picture of how successful an event has been or will be in the future if identified improvements are put into practice.

Skills and knowledge check

☐ I have practised clearing up a room and returning audiovisual equipment and resources.

☐ I can type up meeting notes to produce accurate meeting minutes.

☐ I can analyse and interpret participant feedback to understand where improvements could be made.

☐ I have practised using business technology to produce information relating to the results of participant feedback.

☐ I can present recommendations for improvement of future events.

○ I know which post-event activities I am responsible for.

○ I know what information needs to be circulated to participants following an event.

○ I can describe the different methods for capturing participant feedback and the type of information I should collect.

Ready for assessment

You will need to show you can plan and prepare for a business event in accordance with a given brief.

Agreeing an event brief

Evidence may take the form of a reflective account or an audio recording of a discussion you have had with a tutor, assessor, colleague, supervisor or peer, which confirms your understanding of the event brief.

Planning for an event

Evidence should include draft event plans for different events. You should also provide a reflective account or an audio recording of a discussion you have had with a tutor, assessor, colleague, supervisor or peer, which confirms your considerations in planning the events.

Making preparations for an event in line with agreed brief

Evidence may take the form of internet search outcomes relating to venues, travel and accommodation. Lists of equipment, resources, event material and information relating to guest speakers or presenters would demonstrate understanding of these requirements. Video evidence, photographs or witness testimonies of you setting up rooms ready for business events can also be used, as well as reflective accounts or an audio recording of a discussion you have had with a tutor, assessor, colleague, supervisor or peer, which demonstrates your contingency planning considerations.

Processing and communicating information before and during the event

Evidence may take the form of printed documents, screenshots, photographs, videos or witness testimonies confirming how information has been produced, copied, collated and communicated to participants.

Welcoming and registering participants

You will need to show that you can welcome and register participants who attend the event you are supporting. Evidence may take the form of video evidence, photographs or witness testimonies. Records such as participant registers and name badges would also be appropriate.

Responding to queries, issues, problems and complaints

You may choose to write a reflective account or record a discussion you have had with your tutor, assessor, colleague or supervisor, detailing queries, issues, problems and complaints raised during the event and confirm actions you have taken to resolve them.

Taking and distributing minutes

Evidence may take the form of actual notes made during the event. You will need to show you can take accurate notes that reflect the agenda of the event. Email evidence could be provided to show you have distributed minutes.

Follow-up activities to an event

You will need to show you can carry out post-event activities such as tidying up the room, producing minutes and using and analysing participant feedback. Evidence may take the form of videos, photographs or witness testimonies. Results of feedback could be presented as a slide show or written report which includes recommendations to improve future events.

UNIT 4 | PLANNING, ORGANISING AND SUPPORTING BUSINESS EVENTS

WORK FOCUS

HANDS ON

Skills	Do	Don't
Creating an event plan	<ul><li>agree the event brief before creating the event plan</li><li>identify the requirements early on</li><li>have a plan B</li><li>keep the plan on track</li></ul>	<ul><li>leave anything to chance</li><li>try and plan everything on your own</li></ul>
Sourcing venues, equipment, accommodation and travel	<ul><li>stick to the budget</li><li>select venues, equipment, accommodation and travel which represent value for money</li><li>check venues and hotels have parking and internet access</li><li>get quotes to help stick to the budget</li></ul>	<ul><li>choose dates near holidays or public events</li><li>do it on the cheap</li><li>ignore venue or hotel reviews</li></ul>
Preparing information and materials for participants	<ul><li>publicise the event through all available channels including social media</li><li>send pre-registration information to participants</li><li>check information for accuracy and completeness before communicating to participants</li></ul>	<ul><li>forget to use spellchecker or get information and materials proofread before sending out</li><li>just print them</li></ul>
Setting up a venue to meet event requirements	<ul><li>check equipment and resource requirements of presenters</li><li>select a room layout which best suits the event type</li></ul>	<ul><li>have too much or too little seating or space</li><li>forget about venue set up and take down time</li><li>forget health, safety and security</li></ul>
Taking and producing minutes of a meeting	<ul><li>follow organisational and legal requirements when minute taking</li><li>confirm attendees and non-attendees in advance</li><li>use a copy of the agenda as a guide</li><li>be concise and accurate</li></ul>	<ul><li>forget the legalities</li><li>record discussion unless directed to do so</li><li>be shy in asking for clarification during the meeting</li></ul>
Resolving issues and complaints during an event	<ul><li>stay calm and apologise</li><li>listen to the issue or complaint and ask questions</li><li>use complaints as an opportunity to improve</li><li>work hard to solve the problem</li><li>seek help when you need to</li></ul>	<ul><li>respond with anger</li><li>break promises</li><li>ignore issues and complaints</li></ul>

Ready for work?

Take this short quiz to find out whether you'd be the person chosen for that dream job.

1. When creating an event plan, you should:
   - [ ] A record and prioritise preparation activities
   - [ ] B get your workmate to write it
   - [ ] C keep your plan in your head
   - [ ] D not communicate your plan to others.

2. It is important to confirm roles and responsibilities to:
   - [ ] A ignore instructions
   - [ ] B understand what you have to do and when
   - [ ] C get someone else to do it
   - [ ] D know how not to do something.

3. Meeting minutes should be:
   - [ ] A about how long the meeting will last
   - [ ] B accurate records of meeting outcomes and actions
   - [ ] C circulated three months after the event
   - [ ] D not written at all.

4. When speaking to participants, you should:
   - [ ] A chew gum
   - [ ] B speak clearly and professionally
   - [ ] C look up from your mobile phone
   - [ ] D be rude and disrespectful.

5. If there is a fire at an event you should:
   - [ ] A raise the alarm and evacuate the venue
   - [ ] B go back and get your coat and bag
   - [ ] C run like mad
   - [ ] D put the fire out.

Your score:

If you scored mostly As, you may need to brush up on your event support skills. If you scored mostly Cs or Ds, go back and read the sections on planning, preparation and support. If you scored mostly Bs, you are ready for a role in event planning.

Glossary of key terms

ACCURATE: correct and precise

AGENDA: a schedule of items to be discussed at a meeting

APPROVAL PROCEDURE: the process the organisation uses to check the final version of a document before allowing it to be sent to staff or customers

BACK BOARD: a piece of strong card that is placed at the back of bound documents to provide stability

BACK UP: to securely store and/or restore electronic data

BINDING MACHINE: a machine used to make holes in documents so they can be grouped together to form a booklet

BINDING SPINE COMB BARS: a machine is used to attach a round spiral length of plastic to a batch of documents to hold them together

BOARD OF DIRECTORS: a team of senior members of staff in a company who make plans and decisions to drive the organisation forward

BODY LANGUAGE: physical, non-verbal form of communication in which your body position or gestures convey some feeling or intention

BUDGET: the total amount of money allocated for a specific purpose

CHAIRPERSON: the person responsible for leading a meeting and ensuring it is conducted correctly

CIRCULAR: a document that is circulated within the organization

CODES OF CONDUCT: rules that set out how members of staff are expected to behave in an organisation

COMMUNICATION: the sending of information from one person or group to another person or group, for a given purpose

COMPLIANT: to adhere to rules, regulations, policies and procedures

CONSUMABLES: essential, replaceable items used to run a piece of equipment, such as ink or toner for a printer

CONSUMERS: people who purchase goods and services for their own personal needs

CONTINGENCY: a plan for a possible future event

CORPORATE BRANDING: the promotion of the reputation and image of an organisation, for example, by using a company logo that will become recognised by consumers over a period of time

CUSTOMER RELATIONSHIP MANAGEMENT (CRM) INFORMATION SYSTEM: a database used to record existing customers, old customers and potential new customers

DISCLOSE: to reveal secret or confidential information

DISCRIMINATION: the unfair treatment of a person, racial group or minority

DURABLE SPINE BARS: plastic bars that slide over a collection of documents to hold them together

EMAIL SIGNATURE: the text used to finish your email, usually including your name, contact details and job description

ENCLOSURES: items enclosed with the main document or letter

FACE-TO-FACE: talking to someone in person

FLAT STRUCTURE: an organisation with two or three levels of hierarchy

FREELANCER: a self-employed person

FRONT COVER BOARD: a piece of strong card or thick paper that is used as a cover sheet for bound documents

FUNCTIONAL STRUCTURE: an organisation that allows teams and individuals to become specialist and expert in one particular aspect of the business and its activities

GANTT CHART: a tool that managers can use to measure progress of activities over a period of time

GATEKEEPING: an administrator preventing a visitor from seeing a colleague without an appointment if the visit is not of an urgent nature

GUILLOTINE: a machine used to cut paper to size

HARD COPY: a physical rather than digital copy of a document

HARDWARE: the physical parts or components of a computer system

HIERARCHICAL STRUCTURE: a mix of tall and flat structures, with many layers of management at the top of the organisation and increasing span of control towards the bottom

HIERARCHY: the different levels of supervision and management with varying degrees of authority

HOUSE STYLE: the style of document presentation used by all staff in the organisation, including layout, type and size of font, size of margins, style of headings, position of the company logo, and content of headers and footers

INTERPERSONAL SKILLS: skills relating to the communication and interaction between people

INTRANET: a private network accessible only by an organisation's employees over the Internet

ITINERARY: a travel plan and timetable of activities for a member of staff who is going away on a business trip

JARGON : words that are specific to a profession or group of people that are hard for others to understand

LAMINATOR: a machine used to coat important documents with a protective cover

LANYARD: a cord that allows you to wear a name badge around your neck

LEGAL DOCUMENT: a legally valid document that provides evidence of how the business makes decisions and the actions taken to resolve business issues

LEGALLY BINDING: an agreement that has been consciously made and certain actions are now required

MATRIX STRUCTURE: a team of people brought together from across the organisation with the necessary skills and experience to complete the project successfully

MINUTES: an official record of the discussions and agreed actions from the meeting

MOP UP EVENTS: events that take place after the main event for the benefit of participants who couldn't attend the first time

MOTIONS: the formal proposals put to a meeting

ONLINE BUSINESS TECHNOLOGY: different computing devices and hardware that access a range of software and system applications in the office or remotely from different locations

OPERATING SYSTEM: a program that manages the basic functions of a computer

PA (PERSONAL ASSISTANT): an administrator who works exclusively for one particular person

PARTNERSHIP: a business owned and controlled by two or more people

PATTERN: something that is repeated

PIGEONHOLE: a box with a staff member's name on it where mail and/or documents are placed

POLICY: a document written by managers stating what can or cannot be done within the organisation

PRECAUTIONARY: the measures taken in advance to protect against possible danger or failure

PREVENTATIVE: the measures intended or used to prevent or hinder an unwanted occurrence

PROCEDURE: a document showing a step-by-step set of instructions that should be followed by everyone, so that a task is completed successfully and in the format required by the business

PROCRASTINATE: to put off a task until a later time without good reason

PROXY VOTERS: the meeting members who may delegate their voting powers to others at the meeting

PUBLICISE: make public or announce

QUORUM: the minimum number of members that must be present to make the proceedings of the meeting valid

REFLECTION ACTIVITY: an activity that identifies what went well, what went less well and how event planning, organisation and support could be better next time

RISK ASSESSMENT: the process of assessing the likelihood and seriousness of certain hazards in the workplace

SHARE SCREENS: software that allows a member in the video conference to show other members an open document or window on their screen

SHARED WORKSPACES: allow people in different locations to access and share files online and work collaboratively on business activities for a common purpose

SLANG: informal language and words that are not appropriate for formal communications

SOCIAL NETWORKS: websites that allow users to communicate with each other

SOFTWARE: a collection of instructions for computer programs that allow you to operate the device and related hardware, and to perform computing tasks

SOLE TRADER: a business owned and controlled by one person

SOUNDSTATION: equipment used to project the caller's voice to a group of people

GLOSSARY

SPAN OF CONTROL: the number of staff one person supervises

STAKEHOLDERS: individuals or bodies with an interest in an organisation's activities, such as a bank, government department, customer or supplier

TALL STRUCTURE: an organisation with many levels of hierarchy, many managers and supervisors, each with their own area of responsibility and teams

THE CLOUD: a form of digital storage using remote servers, usually managed by a hosting company

TONE OF VOICE (VERBAL): the volume, pitch and quality of the voice

TONE OF VOICE (WRITTEN): the expressions and language used in the document to reflect the personality and values of the organisation

TREND: something that is popular at a point in time or a change in the way people are behaving

VALIDITY: the extent to which something is genuine or authentic and legally acceptable

VERSION CONTROL: a method of managing multiple variations of the same document so it is clear how the document has developed over time and which is the current version

VIDEO CONFERENCING: software that uses computers with webcams to provide a video link between two or more people, such as Skype®

VISA: an official document that allows a named person to enter, travel through and leave a specified country

Index

A

access to computer files 100
accommodation, booking 63, 139–40
accuracy 21
   of business documents 111
   of data input 66
   of information 98, 102
   of travel arrangements 15
   of written communication 21
active listening 24, 82
administrative activities 54–66
   arranging business trips 63–4
   diaries and appointments 57–60
   information management 65–6
   mail handling 55–7
   receptionist duties 61–2
   supporting meetings 60–1
administrative roles and services 4–19
   business travel 15–17
   document storage 17–19
   mail services 13–15
   meetings 4–7
   office equipment 7–13
administrative service provision 52–87
   assessment 53, 85
   effective communication 81–4
   to meet requirements 68–70
   office equipment 71–6
   professional behaviours 77–81
   routine activities 54–66
   time and workload management 66–8
   work focus 86–7
administrative services 2–50
   assessment 3, 46–50
   legal issues 28–38
   organisational structure 38–44
   roles and services 4–19
   work focus 45
   working relationships 20–7
age discrimination 36

agendas 5, 96
   business events 147, 149, 161
air travel 16
applications software 93–4
   database software 102
   for document production 105–10
   local applications 94–5
   presentation software 109, 110
   spreadsheets 101, 102
   word-processing software 109, 110
   see also software
appointments, managing 57–60
approval procedures 108
attachments to emails 117–18
attendance at events, recording 153
audience needs 106, 123
audience types 124
automated systems 97

B

back boards 73
back ups 18, 19, 92
   cloud storage for 115
banquet (room) layout 143
barcode scanners 73
binding machine 72
binding spine comb bars 73
body language 23, 82, 152, 157, 159, 160
bookings
   for business events 139–40
   business trips 15–16, 63–4
   meeting venue 4–5
branding 83, 108
brief, business events 131–3
budget 5
   event brief 132
business documents see documents
business events 128–74
   administrative support 151–64
   agreeing a brief 130–3
   assessment 129, 172
   follow-up activities 164–71
   information, processing and communicating 147–50

   making preparations for 137–46
   planning for 133–7
   work focus 173–4
business technology
   benefits of using 97–8
   supporting organisations 96–9
   types of 90–5
business travel 15–17, 63–4
   booking travel and accommodation 63
   documentation for travel 64
   making arrangements 15
   problems that can arise 17
   types of travel 16
   use of itineraries 63–4

C

calendar invites, event publicity 148
car travel 16
chairperson 5
charts 168, 169
checking
   content of documents 111–12
   of records 102–3
circulars 55
civil partnership 36
classroom layout 143
cloud storage 114–15
codes of conduct 77
command words, exam questions 46
communication 20, 81–4, 97
   business events 156–7
   with customers and staff 97
   impact of poor 24
   non-verbal 23–4, 82, 157
   planning 83–4
   verbal 20–1, 82, 156–7
   web-based events 123
   written 21–2, 83
Companies Act (2006) 163
complaints
   business events 160–1
   customer 97
   poor communication 24
completeness, checking for 102

INDEX

compliance 68, 123
  with organisational expectations 77–9
  with procedures, regulations and standards 98–9, 123
  web-based events 123
  when saving your work 112–14
computer software 92–4
computer systems 72
computers 8
computing devices 91
computing hardware 91–2
conference (room) layout 143
conferencing, video 90
confidentiality 17–18
  document shredding 12, 78
  incoming mail 55
  and web-based communications 123
consumables 73
Consumer Contracts Regulations (2013) 35
consumer rights 34–5
Consumer Rights Act (2015) 34
consumers 34
contingency plans 17, 123
  business events 136, 146
  web-based events 123
contracts, business events 136
Control of Substances Hazardous to Health Regulations (COSHH) (2002) 33
cooperatives 39
copyright symbol 107
Copyrights, Designs and Patents Act (1988) 107
corporate branding 83, 108
courier services 14
customer communication using technology 97
customer service, business events 153

D

data input 66, 100–1
data management software 100–4
data processing 96
Data Protection Act (1998) 17–18
  principles of personal information use 28
data validation 102–3
database software 101, 102
deadlines 24, 106, 135
descriptive statistics 167–8
desktop computers 91
desktop publishing software 94
diaries, managing 57–60
dietary requirements, event participants 157–8
differences, respecting 80–1
digital content 35
digital storage 114–15
disability discrimination 36
disclosure 14–15, 99
discrimination 36, 155–6
dismissal 37
dispute resolution 38
distractions, dealing with 67–8
document binders 73
document scanners 73
document storage 17–19
  complying with organisational requirements 112–14
  digital storage methods 114–15
  electronic documents, back up of 19
  paper documents, filing methods 18–19
  physical storage methods 115
  security and confidentiality 17–18
documents 96
  for business travel 64
  checking 111–12
  planning 105–6
  printing, collating and distributing 65
  researching information 106–7
  saving 112–14
  software for creating 109–10
  standard layouts and conventions 107–8
  standards and requirements 108
  see also document storage
Dropbox™ 91, 114, 120
durable spine bars 73

E

electronic diaries 57, 58
electronic documents, storage of 19
electronic filing systems 65–6
email queries, responding to 149
email signatures 119
email software 117–19
employee differences, respecting 80–1
employers' and employees' responsibilities 29
Employment Rights Act (1996) 37–8
enclosures 14
Equality Act (2010) 36, 155
equality laws 36–8
equipment
  for business events 141–2
  health and safety issues 33
  for meetings 6
  office 7–13, 71–6
  security of 6
evaluation
  criteria, event brief 132
  event planning 170
  external services 165–6
  of risks 30
event brief 131–2
  importance of agreeing 132–3
event follow-up 164–71
  external services, performance of 165–6
  feedback from participants 166–70
  follow-up activities 165
  future improvements 170
  planning effectiveness, evaluating 170
  post-event activities 164
event planning 133–7
  agreeing the plan 137
  creating a plan 134–6
  issues 136–7
  roles and responsibilities 134
event preparation 137–51
  administrative activities 149
  booking venue, accommodation and travel 139–40
  equipment and resources 141–2
  information requirements 147
  maximum attendance,

achieving 150
participant packs 149–50
potential failures, causes and contingencies 146
publicity 147–8
refreshments 144
rules and regulations 145
sourcing a venue 137–9
speakers and presenters, arranging 142
venue set-up 143
event types 130
event welcome and registration process 151–9
   effective communication 156–7
   greeting event participants 151–2
   health, safety and security 158–9
   issuing name badges 154
   meeting needs of participants 154–6
   personal behaviours and presentation 152–3
   providing refreshments 157–8
   recording attendance 153
extensions to filenames 113, 114

F

face-to-face discussions 20
Facebook 121
failures/problems, business events 146
feedback from customers 97
feedback from event participants 167–70
   analysing 167–8
   collecting 166–7
   patterns and trends 169
   presenting graphically/visually 168–9
   sharing results 169–70
feedback from team members 26, 111
ferry travel 16
file access 100
file storage 103–4
file versions 104
filenames 113
filing cabinets 18–19, 115
filing methods 19
fishbone (room) layout 143
fitness-for-purpose, business

documents 111–12
flat structures 40–1
folders, for computer files, creating 101, 113
follow-up see event follow-up
food and drink see refreshments
food safety 145
franking machines 11, 73
freelancers 37
front cover boards 73
functional structures 43–4

G

Gantt charts 66
gatekeeping role of receptionist 58–9
gender reassignment 36
Google Docs™ 91, 95, 114, 120
Google Hangouts™ 120
graphical presentation of results 168–9
greeting
   event participants 151–2
   meeting attendees 6
guillotines 71, 73

H

handheld scanners 73
hard copy 115
hardware 91–2, 93
health and safety
   business events 158
   employers' and employees' responsibilities 29
   procedures, following 78–9, 98–9
   regulations 31–4
   risk assessment 30
Health and Safety at Work Act (1974) 29, 78
hierarchical structures 42
hierarchy 40
hours of work, regulation on 37
house style 108
'housekeeping' 100
hyperlinks, inserting into emails 119

I

iCloud, Apple® 114
incoming mail 55
individual needs of participants 155–6

infographics 170
information, business event-related 154–5
information collation 100–1
information management 65–6
information needs, business events 147
information processing 97–8
   using data management software 100–4
information research 106–7
information resource facilities 115
information sharing 124, 169–70
information sources, checking validity of 107
information storage 96
information use, Data Protection Act 28–9
input device, choice of 100
inputting data 66
Instagram 122
instant messaging 91, 120–1
intellectual property 107
internal mail 14–15
international mail 13
intranets 116
invitations to meetings 5
   calendar invites to events 148
itineraries 15, 63–4

K

keyboards 92

L

laminators 72, 73
laptops 91
layouts
   of documents 107–8
   of room, business events 143
legal documents 163
legal framework 28–38
   consumer rights 34–5
   equality laws 36–8
   health and safety 29–34
   information use and storage 28–9
legally binding 140
lifting heavy loads 32–3
limited companies 39
LinkedIn 122
listening skills 24, 82

M

mail handling 55–7
  incoming mail 55
  outgoing mail 55–6
  parcels, sending 56–7
mail services 13–15
manual filing systems 65
manual handling, safety issues 32–3
marriage discrimination 36
maternity discrimination 36
matrix structures 43
mean 168
median 168
meetings 60–1
  formal 60
  informal 60
  organising 60–1
  support for 4–7
  see also minutes
messaging 120–1
minutes 7, 96, 161
  different types of 162
  good practice, applying 162
  storing and distributing 163
mode 168
mop up events 150
motions (meeting proposals) 162
mouse 92

N

name of files/folders 113
name badges 147, 154
network drives, sharing 114
networking, social media 90, 121–2, 148
non-verbal communication 23–4, 82, 157
not for profit organisations 39

O

office equipment 7–13, 71–6
  categories of 71–2
  choosing 74
  computers 8
  failure 76
  features 72–4
  franking machines 11
  maintaining 76
  minimising waste 75
  photocopiers/scanners 8–9
  printers 8
  resources 74
  safe working 75
  shredders 12
  telephone system 9–10
  types of 72
online business technology 90
online collaboration software 120–1
online shared workspaces 91
  operating systems 94
operating systems 92
organisational structure
  flat structures 40–1
  functional structures 43–4
  hierarchical structures 42
  matrix structures 43
  and receptionist role 62
  tall structures 41
organisations 38–44
  ownership 38–9
  size 40
  structure 40–4
outgoing mail 13–14
ownership of a business 38–9

P

PA (personal assistant) 59
paper documents, filing methods 18–19
parcels, sending 56–7
participant packs, creating 149–50
partnerships 39
passwords 19
pattern 169
percentages 168
personal behaviours and presentation 152–3
  demonstrating positive 79–81
personal data, principles of processing 28
personal protective equipment (PPE) 31
photocopiers 8–9
photocopying 149
physical storage methods 115
pigeonhole 14
planning
  communication 83–4
  web-based communications 123
  see also event planning
policy 98
positive personal behaviour 79–81
precautionary measures 145
pregnancy 36
presentation software 94, 109–10
preventative measures 145
printers 8, 72, 92
private limited companies 39
private sector 38–9
problems
  business travel 17
  event planning 136
  office equipment 72–3
  using software 103
  see also complaints
procedures 54, 98
professional behaviours 77–81
  health and safety 78–9
  positive personal conduct 79–81
  security procedures 78
professionalism 153
proofreading 22
proxy voters 162
public corporations 39
public limited companies 39
public sector 39
publicity for an event 147–8

Q

quality checking of your work 70
queries, business events 160–1
quorum 162

R

race discrimination 36
range 168
receptionist duties 61–2
recorded delivery 14
records, checking 102–3
redundancy 37
reflection activities 170
refreshments
  for an event 144, 157–8
  providing at meetings 6, 60
registering event participants 153–4
regulations
  anti-discrimination 36–7
  business events 145
  complying with 98–9
  consumer rights 34–5
  health and safety 31–4
  working time directive 37

religious discrimination 36
Reporting of Injuries, Diseases and Dangerous Occurrences Regulations (RIDDOR) (2013) 31
requirements of organisation 68–70
researching information 106–7
resources
   business events 135, 136, 141–2
   for business technology systems 98
   lack of 17
respect 80–1
responsibilities of employers and employees 29
rights
   consumer 34–5
   employment protection 37–8
   equality in employment 37–8
   working hours 37
risk assessment 30
room layout, business events 143

S

safety
   computer use 8
   food 145
   protective clothing 31
   spectator or crowd 145
   when using office equipment 12, 75
   see also health and safety
saving your work 103–4, 112–14
scanners 8–9, 73, 92
screen sharing 90
security
   business events 158–9
   of data 17–18
   of equipment 7
   procedures, following 78
   of stored information 98
service providers, evaluation of 165–6
sex discrimination 36
sexual orientation 36
share screens 91
shared drive workspaces 120
shared network drives 114
shared office equipment 71

shared workspaces 91
SharePoint, Microsoft 91, 95, 114, 120
shredders 12, 73
size of a business 40
Skype™ 90, 120
slang 22
smartphones 91
social media
   for business use 121–2
   event publicity 148
social networks 90
software 92
   applications 93–4
   databases 102
   email 117
   online collaboration 120–1
   presentation 109–10
   problems 103
   spreadsheets 101, 102
   systems 92–3
   word-processing 109–10
sole traders 38
soundstation 72
speakers for events, arranging 142
special delivery 13
speed of information processing 98
spell checking 22, 111
spreadsheets 94, 101, 102
stakeholders 75
standard layouts for documents 107–8
standards of the organisation
   applying to documents 108
   complying with 70, 98–9
stationery 69
statistics, descriptive 167–8
stocktaking 69
storage of documents/information 17–19, 96, 98, 112–16
   data protection issues 28–9
storing and retrieving information 65–6
structure of an organisation 40–4
sub-folders 101
system applications 94–5
systems software 92

T

tablet devices 91
tall structures 41
task briefs 68–9

task preparation 69
teamwork 24–7
   benefits of 26–7
   skills and requirements 25–6
technology 88–127
   assessment 89, 125
   data management software 100–4
   document creation and checking 105–12
   storage of documents 112–16
   supporting organisations 96–9
   types of 90–5
   web-based 116–24
   work focus 126–7
telephone system 9–10
telephone systems 72
ten Cs model, evaluation of service providers 165–6
theatre (room) layout 143
time management techniques 66–7
time off work 37
tone of voice 21, 108
train travel 16
travel see business travel
trends 169
Twitter 122

U

U-shape (room) layout 143

V

validity 102
   of sources 107
   validation checks 102–3
   web-based communications 123
venue for business event
   booking 139–40
   setting up 143
   sourcing 137–9
venues for meetings, booking 4–5
verbal communication 20–1, 82, 156–7
version control 108
video conferencing 90, 121
visas 15
visual display unit (VDU) 92
visual methods of presenting information 168–9

W

wages, legislation 37
waste, minimising 75
web-based applications 95
web-based technology 116–24
  benefits of 123
  email software 117–19
  intranets 116
  issues in planning a web-based event 123–4
  online collaboration software 120–1
  social media 121–2
  target audience 124
WebEx™ 120
whiteboards 134
word-processing software 94, 109–10
working relationships 20–7
  communication 20–4
  teamwork 24–7
Working Time Regulations (1998) 37
workload, techniques for managing 67
workspaces, shared 91
written communication 21–2, 83